Grill It!
Vegetarian

Grill It! Vegetarian

More Than 90 Easy Recipes to Sear, Sizzle, and Savor

Edited by Anne McDowall

PUBLISHED BY
SALAMANDER BOOKS LIMITED
LONDON

A Salamander Book

Published by Salamander Books Ltd.
8 Blenheim Court
Brewery Road
London N7 9NY
United Kingdom

© Salamander Books Ltd., 2002

A member of the Chrysalis Group plc

ISBN 1 84065 369 8

1 3 5 7 9 8 6 4 2

Credits
Commissioning Editor: Stella Caldwell
Project Manager: Anne McDowall
Designer: Mark Holt
Production:Phillip Chamberlain
Colour reproduction: Anorax Imaging Ltd
Printed in China

Contents

Introduction

Gone are the days when barbecues were for meat-eaters only. Modern barbecues have evolved to cater for all contemporary tastes and grilling is great for the vegetarian and anyone else wanting a healthy lifestyle. Not only is food at its best and most flavoursome grilled, but this is also a very healthy way to cook, avoiding the need for extra fat and retaining all the goodness and flavour of the food. It's a particularly good way to cook vegetables, whether cooked on a grill rack, in delicious combinations on skewers, or wrapped in aluminium foil packages and placed directly in the coals.

With a few barbecue basics – a simple barbecue, some fuel and basic tools – plus a grasp of simple barbecue cooking techniques, you'll be set to enjoy not only good food, but also the simple pleasure of cooking and eating outdoors. Once you've mastered a few of the many delicious recipes here, you will feel confident to try some ideas of your own. Remember that cooking over coals isn't an exact science – experimentation is part of its appeal.

Barbecues

There are many different types of barbecue on the market, from simple disposable ones to highly sophisticated gas and electric types and, of course, you can always make your own. If you are new to barbecuing, or about to buy a new one, it's worth taking a few minutes to consider the different options to decide which would suit you best.

We've mentioned the disposable types, but assuming you want to buy something to use more than once, the cheapest and simplest option is a shallow metal bowl on frame (resembling an upturned dustbin lid). There is no venting or cover but it is easy to light and simple to control.

The kettle barbecue has its own hood, often with adjustable ducts, and is suitable for all types of barbecuing. There are several advantages to having a hood on the barbecue; in bad weather it helps protect food while it is cooking and it also prevents spattering and billowing of smoke.

If you like regular barbecues, you might think about building your own – you can use your own materials or buy a ready-to-assemble pack. Either way, the barbecue should have three walls with bars built into the brickwork. Make sure there is enough space for it as a permanent structure in the garden and think carefully about where you site it. It should be far enough away from the house not to be a fire hazard, in a convenient position for people to mill around, and shielded from strong breezes.

Gas barbecues contain either vaporizer bars or lava bricks, which heat in the gas flame and absorb juices dripping from the food as it cooks, thus creating flavour. These barbecues ignite almost instantaneously and require no starter fuel. They retain an even heat and it is possible to have hot coals on one side and moderate on the other if the model has twin switches. Some are very sophisticated wagon models, but all have a gas bottle, which is cumbersome. However, the advantage with this type of barbecue is that you can use it at any time of the year.

Electric barbecues are more popular in some countries than in others. As with gas grills, they depend on lava bricks to produce an even heat – they take about 10 minutes to heat – and are usually

uncovered. Electric barbecues must not be used in the rain but the more sophisticated models can be used indoors with suitable ducting.

Fuel

Unless you are using a gas or electric barbecue, you will also need to buy suitable fuel. There are two types of coal fuel that can be used: lumpwood charcoal is cheaper, easier to light and burns hotter than its alternative, pressed briquettes. However, once briquettes have been lit, they last a lot longer. Wood can also be used as a fuel, but is more difficult to start. If you do want to use wood, choose hardwoods, which burn longer. Allow the flames to die right down before cooking.

Aromatic wood chips are available for use on barbecues to impart flavours to the food. Oak and hickory wood chips are especially popular, but you may also wish to try more unusual ones, such as mesquite and cherry. You will need to soak the wood

Accessories

The right equipment is a great help for easy barbecuing and a few tools are worth investing in. Here are some items that you will find useful:

◆ Wooden block or table – useful for keeping implements and food close to hand
◆ Long tools, including tongs and forks – ordinary kitchen tools are not long enough to keep the hands away from the heat source
◆ Wire baskets, such as rectangular, hinged ones (see below right) – to support the food
◆ Skewers – square metal, long wooden or bamboo ones are best

◆ Brushes – for basting food with oil or marinade
◆ Heavy-duty aluminium foil – for wrapping food to cook in the coals or on the grill rack
◆ Tapers – better than short matches for lighting the barbecue
◆ Oven gloves – but not the double-handed kind
◆ Apron – a thick one with pockets is ideal
◆ Metal griddle plates – for cooking certain fragile food on
◆ Water sprayer – for dousing the flames if they become too unruly
◆ Stiff wire brush and metal scrapers – for cleaning the barbecue

chips for about 30 minutes in cold water, then drain them, before you place them on the ashen coals.

Firelighters, jelly starters or lighting ignition fluid are also essential to start the barbecue. Make sure you follow the manufacturer's instructions carefully if you are using ignition fluid and never use petrol, paraffin or other similar flammable liquids to light a barbecue – apart from affecting the taste of the food they are highly dangerous.

Lighting the barbecue
Before you light the barbecue, ensure that it is in the right position (a hot barbecue is difficult to shift). There is no particular mystique in starting a charcoal fire. Spread a single layer of coals over the barbecue base, pile up the coals a little and push in firelighters or jelly starters. (Don't worry about instructions to make a pyramid, as it really isn't necessary.) Light with a taper, rather than matches, and as soon as the fire has caught, spread the coals out a little and add further pieces as necessary.

The coals will probably take 30-40 minutes to become hot enough to start cooking over; when the flames have died down and the charcoal is covered with a white ash, it is time to commence cooking. (Lava bricks on the other hand only take a few minutes to heat up sufficiently.) Charcoal will burn up for about 1½ hours and occasionally pieces can be added around the edges. Use smaller pieces to poke through spaces in the grid, if necessary.

Checking and adjusting the temperature
Grilling or barbecuing can be done over high, medium or low heat, depending on the type of food. It is easy to adjust the heat on gas and electric barbecues, but more difficult with the open grid types unless you have a kettle barbecue with adjustable vents. To test the temperature of the barbecue, place your open hand over the coals, but be careful when doing so. If you can keep your hand a few inches

above the coals for as long as 5 seconds the temperature is low; for 3-4 seconds it is medium hot, and for only 2 seconds it is hot.

The right height for cooking is about 5-7.5cm (2-3in) above the grid. On a lidded barbecue the heat will be greater when the lid is lowered. If you want to cook over medium heat and the coals have become too hot, either place the food away from the centre of the barbecue and when cooking is completed push it right to the edges to keep warm, or push the coals aside to distribute their heat. To make the fire hotter, poke away the ash, push the coals together and gently blow (you can use a battery operated fan for this – it is invaluable and inexpensive).

Using marinades
Marinating plays a vital part in barbecuing, as it adds depth of flavour. If food has been marinated in the refrigerator, allow it to come back to room temperature before cooking. Marinades that contain acidic elements, such as vinegar or citrus juice, will tenderize the food. Oils in marinades help prevent food from sticking, while herbs and spices create mouthwatering flavours. Marinating can turn even the simplest vegetable into something special.

Cooking in foil
Wrapping food in heavy-duty or double-thickness aluminium foil prevents the outside of the food from burning before the inside is cooked and keeps the juices trapped inside. For foods that require some browning, leave some space between the covering and the food, otherwise wrap into tight packets. Make sure the edges of the foil are firmly sealed.

Cooking in the coals
This is also known as cooking in the embers, and the food can be either wrapped in foil and dropped into the coals, or, in some cases, even placed directly in the coals without any wrapping.

Using skewers

Most skewered food is marinated first. During cooking the food should be brushed either with oil, or with a marinade or baste, and the skewers will need to be turned frequently during cooking. Wooden handles on skewers don't get as hot as metal ones. Look for long skewers, which go fully across the grid and hold enough for 2–3 servings. Make sure wooden handles protrude from the edge of the grid to prevent scorching. Bamboo skewers are good for smaller portions, but need soaking for an hour before you use them, or they will burn. It is generally best to oil metal skewers before use. Serve food on the skewers or transfer onto the plates with a fork.

Grilling

All barbecues can be used for grilling on top of the flame – indeed this is the cooking method generally associated with barbecues. Most of the recipes in this book could also be cooked under a conventional grill if the weather drives you indoors, although the true barbecue flavour will be lacking.

Frying

A heavy-based frying pan or griddle can be used over a barbecue in the same way as on the ordinary cooker hob. Merely grease the surface and the cooking becomes a cross between baking over the barbecue and shallow frying. Should the food start cooking too quickly, just move the pan to the side of the barbecue. Coals need to be very hot for successful barbecue frying.

Cooking times

Although times are given in the recipes, they must be regarded as a guide only. There are so many variables – cooking times will be affected by the thickness of the food, the type and heat of the coals, the position of the rack, the weather, and so on. One of the great pleasures of barbecuing is that it is a chance to experiment.

Cleaning up

When you have finally finished with the barbecue, push the coals away from the centre and they will die down. Cleaning the grill is best done while it is still hot. Use a metal scraper or stiff wire brush to dislodge food residues into the fire. If bits of food remain, remove the grill rack when it is cold and wash in soapy water. When the embers are completely cold, sift away surplus ash and cover the barbecue with the lid for use next time.

Safety checklist

- Always place the barbecue on even ground and away from trees, buildings or fences.
- Never use petrol or similar flammable liquid to light the barbecue, and keep boxes of matches away from the flames.
- Have a bottle of water handy to douse the flames if necessary.
- Once the barbecue is alight, do not leave it unattended and keep children away from it.
- Always use long-handled tongs when handling food on the barbecue.
- Keep food to be barbecued in the refrigerator until you are ready to cook it, then keep it covered and out of the sun.
- Allow embers to cool completely (for several hours) before disposing of them.
- Allow transportable barbecues to cool completely before packing them away.

Starters and Snacks

Radicchio with Mozzarella

SERVES 4

6 ANCHOVIES IN OLIVE OIL

*2 GARLIC CLOVES,
CUT INTO SLIVERS*

*2 LARGE HEADS RADICCHIO,
CUT IN HALF LENGTHWAYS*

SALT AND FRESHLY GROUND BLACK PEPPER

*115G (4OZ) MOZZARELLA CHEESE,
THINLY SLICED*

LEMON SLICES, TO GARNISH

◆ Drain anchovies, reserving oil, and chop. Push garlic slivers and anchovy pieces between radicchio leaves.

◆ Barbecue radicchio halves, cut side up, over medium coals for 5 minutes, or until the underside of the radicchio softens and begins to brown. Remove from the barbecue. Season with salt and pepper.

◆ Place each radicchio half, cut side up, on a piece of double-thickness aluminium foil, drizzle with a little oil reserved from anchovies. Arrange mozzarella slices on top.

◆ Seal packages and replace on grill for 10 minutes, or until mozzarella is melting.

◆ Garnish with lemon slices and serve immediately.

Chive and Garlic Bread

SERVES 6

1 FRENCH STICK

3 GARLIC CLOVES

¼ TEASPOON SALT

115G (4OZ) BUTTER

*2 TABLESPOONS CHOPPED
FRESH CHIVES*

◆ Slice loaf diagonally and deeply at about 2cm (¾in) intervals, but do not cut through completely.

◆ Peel garlic, place on a piece of greaseproof paper, sprinkle with salt and crush with flat side of a table knife. Soften butter, blend in garlic and mix in chives. Spread garlic butter between slices, covering both sides generously.

◆ Reshape the loaf and wrap securely in aluminium foil. Place on rack and barbecue over hot coals for 10-15 minutes, turning parcel over several times. Open foil and serve at once.

Polenta with Vegetables

SERVES 4

SALT AND FRESHLY GROUND BLACK PEPPER

115G (4OZ) POLENTA

15G (½OZ) BUTTER

1 SMALL AUBERGINE, THINLY SLICED

1 COURGETTE, THINLY SLICED

115ML (4FL OZ) OLIVE OIL

1 RED PEPPER, QUARTERED AND SEEDED

BASIL SPRIGS, TO GARNISH

◆ Put 550ml (20fl oz) water in a saucepan and bring to the boil. Add a pinch of salt, then pour in polenta in a fine, steady stream, stirring vigorously with a wooden spoon. Simmer gently for 5-10 minutes, stirring frequently, until polenta is thick and no longer grainy. Remove the pan from the heat and stir in butter and black pepper.

◆ Turn polenta onto an oiled baking sheet or wooden board and spread out to a thickness of 0.5-1cm (¼-½in). Cool, cover and chill for 1 hour. With a 6-7.5cm (2½-3in) pastry cutter, cut polenta into 8 circles.

◆ Brush aubergine and courgette with oil and place on the barbecue until browned on both sides. Keep warm. Barbecue pepper quarters and peel away and dispose of blackened skins. Keep warm.

◆ Brush polenta circles with oil and barbecue for 3-4 minutes on each side until browned and crisp.

◆ Place a polenta circle on each of 4 serving plates and arrange vegetable slices on top. Season with salt and pepper and top with another polenta circle. Garnish with basil to serve.

Tomato and Olive Oil Bruschetta

SERVES 6

6 LARGE RIPE TOMATOES, THINLY SLICED

6 LARGE BASIL LEAVES, SHREDDED

*ABOUT 85ML (3FL OZ)
EXTRA VIRGIN OLIVE OIL*

SALT AND FRESHLY GROUND BLACK PEPPER

*1 SMALL CIABATTA LOAF (ITALIAN OLIVE OIL
BREAD) OR FRENCH STICK*

2 GARLIC CLOVES, HALVED

◆ Place tomatoes, basil, olive oil and seasonings in a dish, stir to combine and leave to marinate for 30 minutes.

◆ Slice bread in half lengthways and toast both sides on the barbecue for 1-2 minutes until lightly golden.

◆ Rub garlic all over toast and top with marinated tomato mixture. Cut into fingers and serve.

Tofu with Miso Sauce

SERVES 4

500G (1LB 2OZ) (2 CAKES)
FIRM COTTON TOFU

TOASTED SESAME SEEDS,
TO SPRINKLE

BAMBOO LEAVES,
TO GARNISH (OPTIONAL)

MISO SAUCE

100G (3½OZ) MISO

1 EGG YOLK

1 TABLESPOON SAKE

1 TABLESPOON MIRIN

1 TABLESPOON SUGAR

4 TABLESPOONS DASHI
(SEE NOTE)

JUICE ¼ LIME

◆ Wrap each tofu cake in a tea towel and place a light weight, such as a plate, on top to squeeze out water. Leave to stand for at least 1 hour.

◆ To make miso sauce, place miso in a bowl and blend in egg yolk, sake, mirin and sugar. Place bowl over a saucepan of simmering water.

◆ Gradually add dashi to pan and stir until sauce becomes thick but not too hard, then stir in lime juice.

◆ Remove from heat immediately and cool to room temperature (it will keep well in the refrigerator, if wished).

◆ Unwrap tofu cakes and cut into 5 x 2 x 1cm (2 x ¾ x ½in) slices. Skewer each of the slices lengthways with 2 bamboo skewers. Place on the barbecue rack over hot coals for a few minutes until lightly browned on one side only.

◆ Remove from heat and, using a butter knife, thickly spread toasted side with miso sauce. Sprinkle with toasted sesame seeds.

◆ Place skewers on barbecue again for 1-2 minutes. Serve hot on skewers on a bed of bamboo leaves as a garnish.

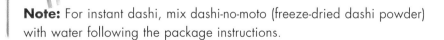

Note: For instant dashi, mix dashi-no-moto (freeze-dried dashi powder) with water following the package instructions.

North African Stuffed Vine Leaves

SERVES 4

1 TABLESPOON CHOPPED FRESH MINT

¼ TEASPOON GROUND CORIANDER

PINCH GROUND CUMIN

SALT AND FRESHLY GROUND BLACK PEPPER

*4 SPRING ONIONS,
FINELY CHOPPED*

*1 SMALL NECTARINE OR PEACH,
STONED AND FINELY CHOPPED*

8 LARGE VINE LEAVES

OLIVE OIL, FOR BRUSHING

*115G (4OZ) GOAT'S CHEESE
OR LOW-FAT CREAM CHEESE*

*CRISP GREEN SALAD, TO SERVE
(OPTIONAL)*

◆ In a small bowl, mix together mint, ground coriander, ground cumin and salt and pepper. Add spring onions and nectarine or peach and stir well to coat evenly in spice mixture.

◆ Wash and dry vine leaves, arrange in pairs on serving plates and brush top leaves with olive oil.

◆ Cut cheese into 4 equal slices. Place a slice of cheese at one end of each pair of leaves and top with nectarine mixture.

◆ Carefully fold leaves over cheese until completely covered and secure with cocktail sticks.

◆ Brush parcels with oil, place on the rack and barbecue over hot coals for 4-5 minutes.

◆ Transfer to serving plates, carefully remove cocktail sticks and serve at once with a crisp green salad.

Grilled Goat's Cheese

SERVES 4

2 TABLESPOONS OLIVE OIL

2 TABLESPOONS WALNUT OR HAZELNUT OIL

1 TEASPOON BLACK PEPPERCORNS,
COARSELY CRUSHED

1 TABLESPOON CHOPPED FRESH THYME

4 GOAT'S CHEESES OR 4 SLICES
GOAT'S CHEESE

225G (8OZ) FRISÉE LETTUCE

25G (1OZ) ROCKET

4 THIN SLICES FRENCH BREAD

1 TABLESPOON RED WINE VINEGAR

½ TEASPOON DIJON MUSTARD

◆ Mix together olive and walnut (or hazelnut) oils, peppercorns and thyme. Put cheese in a small shallow dish, pour over oil mixture and turn cheese in oil to coat.

◆ Leave to marinate in refrigerator for 12-14 hours, turning cheese occasionally.

◆ Arrange frisée and rocket on serving plates. Remove cheese from oil to a plate, reserving oil.

◆ Brush both sides of each slice of bread with a little reserved oil. Toast one side of bread over a hot barbecue.

◆ Remove from the rack and top toasted side with cheese. Replace on the rack over hot coals until cheese is beginning to melt.

◆ Whisk together vinegar and mustard then slowly whisk in reserved oil. Pour over salad leaves, top with grilled goat's cheese and serve immediately.

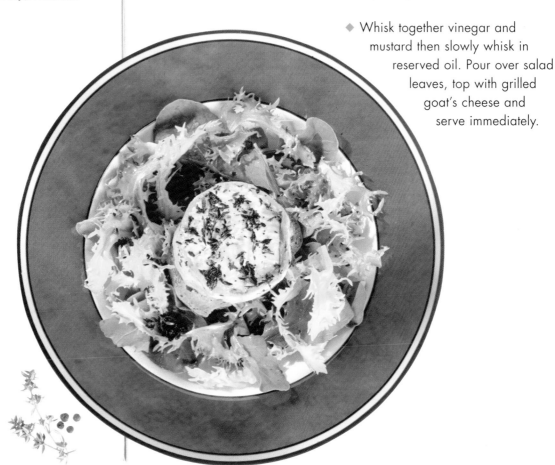

Goat's Cheese, Leek and Walnut Bruschetta

*6 SLICES FRENCH BREAD,
SLICED DIAGONALLY*

3 TABLESPOONS OLIVE OIL

*6 x 45G (1½ OZ) SLICES SOFT
GOAT'S CHEESE*

FRESHLY GROUND BLACK PEPPER

LEEK AND WALNUT TOPPING

2 TABLESPOONS OLIVE OIL

*85G (3OZ) LEEKS,
THINLY SLICED*

*15G (½OZ) WALNUTS,
COARSELY CHOPPED*

◆ To make topping, heat oil in a saucepan and sauté leeks for about 3 minutes until soft.

◆ Remove from heat, stir in chopped walnuts and season with salt and pepper to taste. Set aside until required.

◆ Brush both sides of bread slices with 2 tablespoons of olive oil. Place bread on the barbecue rack over hot coals and toast for about 2 minutes on one side only.

◆ Remove from the barbecue and divide leek and walnut topping between toasted sides of bread slices. Top each with a slice of goat's cheese and drizzle with remaining olive oil. Grind over some black pepper.

◆ Return bruschetta to barbecue and cook for a further 3-4 minutes until cheese begins to melt. Serve at once.

Crispy Potato Skins

SERVES 5-8

4 LARGE BAKING POTATOES

115G (4OZ) BUTTER

SALT AND FRESHLY GROUND BLACK PEPPER

◆ Scrub potatoes and pat dry with paper towels. Prick skin in several places, wrap tightly in aluminium foil and barbecue directly in hot coals for 45 minutes to 1 hour.

◆ Halve potatoes lengthways and scoop out flesh. (Save to use for mashing, or for potato salad if firm enough.) Cut potato skins into 2.5cm (1in) wide strips.

◆ Melt butter and season to taste with salt and pepper. Dip potato skins into melted butter, then thread onto skewers and cook on the barbecue rack over hot coals for 5-7 minutes.

◆ Serve hot.

Peanut Tomatoes

SERVES 4-8

8 SLICES WHITE BREAD

4 BEEF TOMATOES

SALT AND FRESHLY GROUND
BLACK PEPPER

FEW DROPS WORCESTERSHIRE SAUCE

2 TEASPOONS CHOPPED
FRESH BASIL

2 TEASPOONS CHOPPED
FRESH PARSLEY

1 TABLESPOON GRATED
PARMESAN CHEESE

55G (2OZ) ROASTED UNSALTED PEANUTS,
FINELY GROUND

1 TABLESPOON BUTTER

BASIL OR PARSLEY SPRIGS,
TO GARNISH

◆ To make fried croûton 'bracelets', cut 8 rounds from slices of bread and use a slightly smaller cutter to remove centres. Shallow-fry in oil. Drain thoroughly and set aside. (These can be made ahead of time, frozen, and re-crisped on the barbecue at the last minute.)

◆ Rinse and dry tomatoes and halve crossways. Season cut surfaces of tomatoes with salt and pepper. Sprinkle with a few drops of Worcestershire sauce.

◆ Top tomatoes with basil and parsley mixed together, then sprinkle with grated Parmesan cheese. Cover with ground peanuts and add a small knob of butter to each one.

◆ Loosely wrap tomato halves separately in single-thickness aluminium foil. Place cut sides up on the rack and barbecue over hot coals for 20-25 minutes until tomatoes are soft.

◆ Remove from foil wrappings and place each tomato in centre of a fried croûton bracelet. Garnish with basil or parsley sprigs.

Aubergine and Cheese Parcels

1 LARGE AUBERGINE

115ML (4FL OZ) EXTRA VIRGIN OLIVE OIL

SALT AND FRESHLY GROUND BLACK PEPPER

*2 CIABATTA LOAVES
(ITALIAN OLIVE OIL BREAD)
OR 2 FRENCH STICKS*

*2 TABLESPOONS CHOPPED
FRESH BASIL*

2 RIPE PLUM TOMATOES

115G (4OZ) MOZZARELLA CHEESE

◆ Remove and discard stalk from aubergine and slice lengthways into 4 long slices, discarding 2 outer edges (you should be left with 4 flat pieces).

◆ Brush each piece on both sides with half the olive oil and season well with salt and pepper.

◆ Cook aubergine slices on the barbecue for a few minutes on each side until pale golden and soft.

◆ Slice each loaf lengthways in 2, then into 4 chunks. Mix together basil and remaining olive oil and use to brush cut sides of bread.

◆ Slice each tomato into 4 and cut mozzarella into 4 thick slices. Layer tomato and mozzarella to produce 4 stacks, each consisting of one piece of cheese sandwiched between 2 slices of tomato.

◆ Wrap a slice of aubergine around each cheese and tomato stack and place each parcel between 2 pieces of ciabatta bread.

◆ Wrap each parcel in a piece of aluminium foil, turning over edges to seal in filling.

◆ Place parcels on the rack over hot coals and barbecue for 4-5 minutes on each side until bread is warmed through and cheese has begun to melt. Serve at once.

Fennel with Feta and Pears

SERVES 4

2 FENNEL BULBS

4 TABLESPOONS OLIVE OIL

175G (6OZ) FETA CHEESE

1 RIPE PEAR

*4 SUN-DRIED TOMATOES IN OIL,
DRAINED AND SLICED*

8 STONED BLACK OLIVES

*1 TABLESPOON BASIL LEAVES,
SHREDDED*

1 TEASPOON LEMON JUICE

½ TEASPOON CLEAR HONEY

SALT AND FRESHLY GROUND BLACK PEPPER

◆ Trim fennel, discarding any damaged outer leaves. Cut each bulb lengthways into 6 thin slices.

◆ Brush fennel slices with a little of olive oil, place on grill rack and barbecue for 2-3 minutes on each side until browned and just tender. Leave to cool slightly.

◆ Slice feta into thin slabs and quarter, core and thinly slice pear. Arrange fennel, cheese and pear on serving plates and top with tomatoes, olives and basil.

◆ Blend remaining oil, lemon juice, honey and seasonings together, drizzle over salad and serve.

Vine Leaves with Feta, Olives and Tomatoes

SERVES 4

8 LARGE VINE LEAVES

2 TABLESPOONS OLIVE OIL

*115G (4OZ) FETA CHEESE,
CUT INTO SMALL CUBES*

16 SMALL BLACK OLIVES

8 CHERRY TOMATOES, HALVED

8 SPRIGS FRESH OREGANO

FRESHLY GROUND BLACK PEPPER

◆ Rinse vine leaves and dry them on paper towels. Lay them flat on a surface and brush each leaf with a little olive oil.

◆ Divide feta, black olives, tomatoes and oregano evenly between leaves, placing them in the centre of each leaf. Grind over some black pepper and fold leaves around filling to enclose it completely. Secure vine-leaf parcels with cocktail sticks.

◆ Brush outside of parcels with remaining oil and cook them on a prepared barbecue for about 4-5 minutes, until cheese has begun to melt. (They do not need to be turned, but do keep skewered side of parcels upright, away from coals.)

◆ Serve 2 vine-leaf parcels to each person. Peel away vine leaves and eat filling. (The leaves are purely to enclose filling and are not intended to be eaten.)

Stuffed Chillies

SERVES 4-6

12 LARGE FRESH RED OR GREEN CHILLIES

4 SUN-DRIED TOMATOES IN OIL, DRAINED
AND FINELY CHOPPED

150G (5OZ) MILD SOFT GOAT'S CHEESE

2 SPRING ONIONS, WHITE PART ONLY,
FINELY CHOPPED

2 TEASPOONS FINELY CHOPPED FRESH MINT

1 TEASPOON FINELY CHOPPED FRESH BASIL

SALT AND FRESHLY GROUND BLACK PEPPER

3 TABLESPOONS EXTRA VIRGIN OLIVE OIL

1 TABLESPOON WHITE WINE VINEGAR

FRESH MINT LEAVES, TO GARNISH

◆ Barbecue chillies on the rack over hot coals for 5-8 minutes, turning occasionally, until skins are evenly blistered and charred. Transfer to a plastic bag for a few minutes then peel away and discard skins.

◆ Make a slit along length of each chilli. Carefully rinse off seeds under cold running water. Pat chillies dry with paper towels.

◆ To make filling, in a small bowl, mix together sun-dried tomatoes, goat's cheese, spring onions, mint, basil, salt and pepper.

◆ Divide filling between chillies and arrange on a serving plate. Drizzle over olive oil and vinegar.

◆ Chill in refrigerator for at least 30 minutes before serving, garnished with mint leaves.

Moroccan Spiced Garlic Bread

SERVES 6

2 SMALL FRENCH STICKS

175G (6OZ) BUTTER, SOFTENED

2 GARLIC CLOVES, CRUSHED

1 TABLESPOON TOMATO PURÉE

1 TABLESPOON CHOPPED
FRESH CORIANDER

1 TABLESPOON CHOPPED FRESH PARSLEY

½ TEASPOON GROUND CUMIN

½ TEASPOON GROUND PAPRIKA

PINCH CAYENNE PEPPER

SALT, TO TASTE

◆ Cut bread into 1cm (½in) slices, without cutting right through.

◆ Cream together butter, garlic, tomato purée, coriander, parsley, cumin, paprika, cayenne pepper and salt. Spread a little of this spiced butter between each bread slice. Spread any remaining butter all over bread.

◆ Wrap bread sticks in aluminium foil and turn edges over to seal.

◆ Place foil parcels at the edges of the grill rack and barbecue over hot coals for 5 minutes. Turn parcels over and cook for a further 5 minutes.

◆ Serve piping hot.

Feta Cheese Kebabs

MAKES 24

200G (7OZ) FETA CHEESE

¼ RED PEPPER

¼ YELLOW PEPPER

1 COURGETTE

¼ AUBERGINE

THYME SPRIGS, TO GARNISH

MARINADE

1½ TABLESPOONS OLIVE OIL

1 TABLESPOON RASPBERRY VINEGAR

1 TEASPOON PINK PEPPERCORNS,
CRUSHED

1 TEASPOON CLEAR HONEY

½ TEASPOON DIJON MUSTARD

2 TEASPOONS CHOPPED FRESH THYME

¼ TEASPOON SALT

½ TEASPOON FRESHLY GROUND
BLACK PEPPER

◆ To make marinade, place olive oil, vinegar, pink peppercorns, honey, mustard, thyme, salt and pepper in a large bowl. Stir mixture together with a wooden spoon until thoroughly blended.

◆ Cut feta cheese, peppers, courgette, and aubergine into bite-sized pieces. Add to marinade, stir well to coat evenly, cover with plastic wrap and leave in a cool place for at least 1 hour.

◆ Thread one piece of each ingredient onto wooden cocktail sticks. Just before serving, cook on the barbecue for 2-3 minutes until vegetables are just tender.

◆ Arrange on a serving plate, garnished with sprigs of thyme.

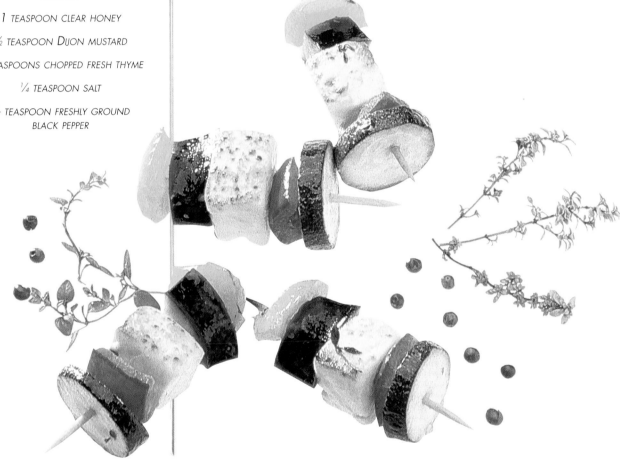

Aubergine, Mushroom and Hazelnut Salad

SERVES 4

1 SMALL AUBERGINE

3 TABLESPOONS OLIVE OIL

115G (4OZ) SHIITAKE MUSHROOMS, WIPED

450G (1LB) MIXED SALAD LEAVES

1½ TABLESPOONS CHOPPED FRESH CORIANDER

25G (1OZ) HAZELNUTS, TOASTED AND COARSELY CHOPPED

DRESSING

85ML (3FL OZ) OLIVE OIL

1 TEASPOON SESAME OIL

2 TEASPOONS LIGHT SOY SAUCE

1 TABLESPOON BALSAMIC VINEGAR

½ TEASPOON SUGAR

FRESHLY GROUND BLACK PEPPER

◆ Cut aubergine into thin slices, brush with oil and cook on the barbecue for 2-3 minutes on each side, until charred and softened. Allow to cool.

◆ Thinly slice mushrooms. Heat remaining oil in a small frying pan and stir-fry mushrooms over a medium heat for 3-4 minutes until tender. Drain on paper towels and leave to cool.

◆ Wash salad leaves, shake off excess water and place in a large bowl. Sprinkle over coriander and nuts.

◆ To make dressing, blend together olive and sesame oils, soy sauce, balsamic vinegar, sugar and black pepper until well mixed.

◆ Add aubergine and mushrooms to salad, pour over dressing, toss well and serve at once.

Vegetables

Chargrilled Artichokes

70ML (2½ FL OZ) OLIVE OIL

1 GARLIC CLOVE,
CRUSHED

2 TABLESPOONS CHOPPED
FRESH PARSLEY

SALT AND FRESHLY GROUND BLACK PEPPER

6 BABY ARTICHOKES

FLAT-LEAF PARSLEY SPRIGS,
TO GARNISH

RED PEPPER SAUCE

1 TABLESPOON OLIVE OIL

1 SMALL ONION, CHOPPED

2 RED PEPPERS, DICED

250ML (9FL OZ) VEGETABLE STOCK

◆ In a small bowl, mix together olive oil, garlic, parsley and salt and pepper. Set aside.

◆ To make red pepper sauce, heat oil in a saucepan, add onion and cook for 5 minutes until soft.

◆ Add red peppers and cook over a low heat for 5 minutes, then pour in stock, bring to boil and simmer for 10 minutes.

◆ Push peppers through a sieve or purée in a food processor or blender. Season with salt and freshly ground black pepper to taste.

◆ Trim bases of artichokes and remove any tough outer leaves. Cut artichokes in half lengthways and immediately brush with seasoned oil.

◆ Lay artichoke halves on a wire rack over medium coals and barbecue for about 10 minutes, turning once, until browned on both sides.

◆ Reheat sauce. Drizzle artichokes with remaining seasoned oil, garnish with parsley and serve with red pepper sauce.

Greek Grilled Vegetables

SERVES 4

2 BABY AUBERGINES

4 BABY COURGETTES

1 RED PEPPER

1 YELLOW PEPPER

1 FENNEL BULB

115G (4OZ) FETA CHEESE

1 TABLESPOON LEMON JUICE

SALT AND FRESHLY GROUND BLACK PEPPER

*COURGETTE FLOWERS,
TO GARNISH*

MARINADE:

150ML (5FL OZ) OLIVE OIL

2 GARLIC CLOVES, CRUSHED

1 TEASPOON CHOPPED FRESH PARSLEY

1 TEASPOON CHOPPED FRESH MINT

*1 TEASPOON CHOPPED
FRESH OREGANO*

◆ To make marinade, mix together olive oil, garlic, parsley, mint and oregano in a small bowl.

◆ Cut aubergines and courgettes lengthways in half. Cut peppers into quarters and remove seeds. Quarter and slice fennel.

◆ Cut feta into small cubes and place in a bowl. Add a little of the marinade and mix gently.

◆ Place aubergines, courgettes, pepper and fennel in another bowl with remaining marinade, mix together and leave for 1 hour.

◆ Barbecue vegetables, turning and brushing with marinade every few minutes, for 10 minutes, or until tender and flecked brown. Leave to cool.

◆ Arrange vegetables on a serving plate. Drizzle with lemon juice and season with salt and pepper. Scatter over feta, garnish with courgette flowers and serve.

Vegetables with Skordalia

*2 YELLOW OR RED PEPPERS,
SEEDED AND QUARTERED*

*225G (8OZ) RAW BEETROOT,
SCRUBBED AND THINLY SLICED*

*225G (8OZ) JERUSALEM ARTICHOKES,
SCRUBBED AND THINLY SLICED*

1 AUBERGINE, THINLY SLICED

*2 SMALL COURGETTES,
SLICED LENGTHWAYS*

*1 SMALL HEAD RADICCHIO,
CUT INTO THIN WEDGES*

*1 FENNEL BULB,
THINLY SLICED LENGTHWAYS*

*225G (8OZ) ASPARAGUS SPEARS,
TRIMMED*

*50ML (2FL OZ) LEMON CITRUS OIL
(SEE NOTE) OR OLIVE OIL*

*1 QUANTITY (225ML/8FL OZ) SKORDALIA
(SEE PAGE 90)*

◆ Brush all vegetables with citrus or olive oil and barbecue over hot coals until charred and tender. (The cooking times will vary depending on the vegetable.)

◆ Arrange vegetables on a large platter and drizzle over any remaining oil. Serve at room temperature with skordalia.

Note: Citrus oil is easy to make but is best made in advance to allow flavours to infuse. Place 4 strips of lemon zest into a clean jar and pour over 300ml (10fl oz) olive oil. It will keep for up to two weeks if stored in the refrigerator.

Chargrilled Peppers

SERVES 6

*6 LARGE PEPPERS,
RED, YELLOW AND ORANGE*

DRESSING

*55ML (2FL OZ) HAZELNUT
OR OLIVE OIL*

2 TEASPOONS BALSAMIC VINEGAR

*1 LARGE GARLIC CLOVE,
CHOPPED*

SALT AND FRESHLY GROUND BLACK PEPPER

*2 TABLESPOONS CHOPPED
FRESH BASIL*

◆ Place peppers on a rack over hot coals and barbecue, turning frequently until skins blister and become charred.

◆ Place peppers in a plastic bag and leave to cool and soften for 30 minutes.

◆ Peel peppers and discard skins and seeds, over a bowl to reserve juices. Cut flesh into thick slices.

◆ Pour pepper juices into a bowl and blend in hazelnut or olive oil, balsamic vinegar, garlic, salt and freshly ground black pepper.

◆ Pour dressing over peppers and sprinkle over basil. Serve peppers warm or cold.

Capered New Potatoes

SERVES 4-6

450G (1LB) NEW POTATOES

3 TABLESPOONS CAPERS

85G (3OZ) BUTTER, SOFTENED

PARSLEY SPRIGS, TO GARNISH

◆ Scrub potatoes well, then boil in their skins in salted water for 10 minutes. Drain and leave to cool slightly.

◆ Finely chop capers and blend with butter. Make a deep slit in each potato and fill with caper butter.

◆ Tightly wrap each potato in individual squares of single-thickness aluminium foil and barbecue on a rack over hot coals for 10-15 minutes.

◆ Garnish with sprigs of parsley to serve.

Baked Sweet Potatoes with Garlic and Thyme

SERVES 4

700G (1½LB) SWEET POTATOES,
PEELED AND CUT INTO SMALL CHUNKS

12 UNPEELED GARLIC CLOVES

12 SPRIGS THYME

85G (3OZ) BUTTER, DICED

SALT AND FRESHLY GROUND BLACK PEPPER

◆ Cut 6 large squares of double-thickness aluminium foil. Divide potatoes between the foil squares. To each pile of potatoes add 2 garlic cloves, 2 sprigs thyme, a few knobs of butter and plenty salt and pepper.

◆ Pull the edges of the foil up and over the potatoes to completely seal the fillings.

◆ Place the parcels over a hot barbecue and cook for 20-25 minutes, until the potatoes are tender. Serve straight from the foil.

Foil-baked Mushrooms

SERVES 6

18 SMALL FLAT-CAP MUSHROOMS

85G (3OZ) BUTTER, SOFTENED

1 GARLIC CLOVE, CRUSHED

1 TABLESPOON CHOPPED
FRESH SAGE

GRATED ZEST 1 LEMON

SALT AND FRESHLY GROUND BLACK PEPPER

◆ Cut 6 large squares of double-thickness aluminium foil. Place 3 mushrooms in the centre of each double layer of foil.

◆ Cream together butter, garlic, sage, lemon zest and salt and pepper and spread about a heaped teaspoonful over each mushroom.

◆ Pull the edges of the foil up over the mushrooms and turn over to seal fillings.

◆ Place the foil parcels over a hot barbecue for 6-8 minutes until mushrooms are tender and juicy. Serve straight from the foil.

Yams and Plantains with Hot Pepper Mayonnaise

SERVES 4

4 x 150G (5OZ) SLICES YAM,
PEELED

4 x 85G (3OZ) THICK SLICES
HALF-RIPE PLANTAIN,
WITH SKINS LEFT INTACT

CORN OIL, FOR BRUSHING

SALT AND FRESHLY GROUND BLACK PEPPER

HOT PEPPER MAYONNAISE

85ML (3FL OZ) MAYONNAISE

2 TABLESPOONS CHOPPED
FRESH THYME

1 TEASPOON SEEDED AND
FINELY CHOPPED HOT JAMAICAN CHILLI

1 TABLESPOON FRESHLY SQUEEZED
LIME JUICE

SALT AND FRESHLY GROUND BLACK PEPPER

◆ Cook yam slices in boiling salted water for 15 minutes or until tender. Drain and set aside until required.

◆ To make hot pepper mayonnaise, mix together in a bowl mayonnaise, thyme, chilli, lime juice, salt and pepper. Refrigerate until required.

◆ Brush yam and plantain slices all over with corn oil and season with salt and freshly ground black pepper.

◆ Cook vegetable slices on the rack of a barbecue, over hot coals, turning them occasionally until they are tender and charred on the outside. The plantains will be ready to serve in about 12 minutes and the yams in about 15.

◆ Serve at once with hot pepper mayonnaise.

Vegetables with Tahini Dressing

SERVES 4

*350G (12OZ) SWEET POTATO,
PEELED AND CUT INTO 4 SLICES*

*450G (1LB) CELERIAC,
PEELED AND CUT INTO 4 SLICES*

*350G (12OZ) PUMPKIN,
PEELED AND CUT INTO 4 WEDGES*

*2 MEDIUM PARSNIPS,
PEELED AND HALVED LENGTHWAYS*

*85ML (3FL OZ) OLIVE OIL
FOR BRUSHING*

SALT AND FRESHLY GROUND BLACK PEPPER

TAHINI DRESSING

3 TABLESPOONS LIGHT TAHINI

3 TABLESPOONS MAYONNAISE

2 TABLESPOONS OLIVE OIL

¼ TEASPOON PAPRIKA

*2 GARLIC CLOVES,
CRUSHED*

*2 SPRING ONIONS,
CHOPPED*

2 TEASPOONS LEMON JUICE

*SALT AND FRESHLY GROUND
BLACK PEPPER*

◆ To make tahini dressing, mix together in a bowl light tahini, mayonnaise, olive oil, paprika, garlic, spring onions, lemon juice, salt and pepper. Refrigerate until required.

◆ Cook different types of root vegetables individually in boiling water until they are just tender. Celeriac will take about 12 minutes to cook, sweet potato 10 minutes, parsnip 8 minutes and pumpkin 6 minutes. Drain cooked vegetables and dry them on paper towels.

◆ Brush vegetables all over with olive oil and season generously with salt and freshly ground black pepper.

◆ Cook vegetables on the oiled rack of the barbecue over hot coals for about 6 minutes on each side, turning them halfway through cooking and brushing occasionally with oil.

◆ Serve with tahini dressing.

Sesame Courgettes

SERVES 6

6 LARGE COURGETTES

SESAME OIL, TO BRUSH

DRESSING

85ML (3FL OZ) SESAME OIL

2 TABLESPOONS LEMON JUICE

*1 TABLESPOON CHOPPED
FRESH ROSEMARY*

PINCH SUGAR

SALT AND FRESHLY GROUND BLACK PEPPER

◆ To make dressing, blend together sesame oil, lemon juice, rosemary, sugar, salt and pepper.

◆ Cut each courgette into 4 thick slices and brush with sesame oil.

◆ Cook courgettes on a rack over hot coals for 2-3 minutes on each side until browned.

◆ Place in a shallow serving dish and pour over dressing. Serve courgettes hot or cold.

Whole Tomatoes in Wine

SERVES 8

8 FIRM TOMATOES

8 TEASPOONS RED WINE

SALT AND FRESHLY GROUND BLACK PEPPER

*WATERCRESS OR LETTUCE LEAVES,
TO SERVE*

◆ Cut 8 large squares of double-thickness aluminium foil. Cup each tomato in foil but do not completely enclose.

◆ Pour 1 teaspoon wine over each tomato and season each to taste with salt and pepper. Mould foil around tomatoes to prevent juices escaping.

◆ Place foil parcels on the side of the rack over medium coals and cook for about 10-15 minutes. Unwrap and transfer to serving plates, spooning wine-flavoured juices over tomatoes.

◆ Serve on a bed of watercress or lettuce leaves.

Japanese Grilled Aubergine

4 AUBERGINES,
STEMS REMOVED

VEGETABLE OIL,
FOR FRYING

4-5CM (1½-2IN) PIECE FRESH ROOT
GINGER, PEELED AND GRATED

8 FRESH MINT LEAVES,
FINELY SHREDDED

GINGER SAUCE

70ML (2½ FL OZ) DASHI
(SEE NOTE)

2 TABLESPOONS SHOYU

2 TABLESPOONS MIRIN
OR 2 TEASPOONS SUGAR

2 TABLESPOONS SAKE

SESAME SAUCE

3 TABLESPOONS WHITE SESAME SEEDS

3 TABLESPOONS DASHI
(SEE NOTE)

1½ TABLESPOONS SHOYU

½ TABLESPOON SUGAR

PINCH SALT

◆ To make ginger sauce, place dashi, shoyu, mirin or sugar and sake in a saucepan and boil for 1 minute. Remove from heat and set aside.

◆ To make sesame sauce, toast sesame seeds in a small dry saucepan, then grind them into a paste in a mortar. Mix in dashi and shoyu and season with sugar and a pinch of salt.

◆ Slice aubergines lengthways into quarters and cook on the rack of a barbecue over hot coals for a few minutes on each side until softened.

◆ Place 2 aubergine slices on each of 8 small plates. Arrange grated ginger and mint slices on top of 4 of the plates and add ginger sauce. Pour sesame sauce over aubergine slices on the other 4 plates. Serve one of each type to each person.

Note: For instant dashi, mix dashi-no-moto (freeze-dried dashi powder) with water following the package instructions.

Spiced Sweetcorn

*4 SWEETCORN,
HUSKS REMOVED*

2 TABLESPOONS OLIVE OIL

½ TEASPOON CAYENNE PEPPER

SALT AND FRESHLY GROUND BLACK PEPPER

CHILLI BUTTER

75G (3OZ) BUTTER, SOFTENED

*2 TABLESPOONS COARSELY CHOPPED
FRESH CORIANDER*

*2 TEASPOONS FINELY CHOPPED
FRESH RED CHILLI*

SALT AND FRESHLY GROUND BLACK PEPPER

◆ To prepare chilli butter, mix together softened butter, coriander, chilli, salt and pepper in a small bowl until thoroughly combined.

◆ Roll butter into a sausage shape on a piece of plastic wrap or greaseproof paper. Roll up to form a cylinder and refrigerate to harden butter.

◆ Cook sweetcorn in plenty of boiling, salted water for about 15 minutes until it is tender, then drain.

◆ In a bowl mix together olive oil, cayenne and seasoning. Brush sweetcorn in flavoured oil to coat.

◆ Cook sweetcorn on the barbecue over hot coals for 10-15 minutes, turning occasionally while cooking. They are ready to serve when they are slightly charred. Serve hot with discs of chilli butter.

Vegetables with Herb and Garlic Oil

SERVES 4-6

4 SWEETCORN

8 BABY FENNEL BULBS

4 PLUM TOMATOES

2 RED ONIONS

2 PEPPERS, GREEN, RED OR YELLOW

HERB AND GARLIC OIL

150ML (5FL OZ) EXTRA VIRGIN OLIVE OIL

2 TABLESPOONS BALSAMIC VINEGAR

2 GARLIC CLOVES, CRUSHED

*8 TABLESPOONS CHOPPED FRESH MIXED HERBS
(E.G. FENNEL, CHIVES, PARSLEY, BASIL)*

SALT AND FRESHLY GROUND BLACK PEPPER

◆ Prepare vegetables for barbecuing. Peel back husks from sweetcorn and knot them at the base. Remove all threads from sweetcorn and discard.

◆ Trim baby fennel and halve tomatoes. Halve onions, leaving skins intact. Halve peppers lengthways and remove cores and seeds, leaving stalks intact.

◆ To make herb and garlic oil, mix together olive oil, balsamic vinegar, garlic and fresh mixed herbs and season to taste with salt and pepper.

◆ Brush vegetables liberally with herb oil and cook on the barbecue, turning and brushing frequently until they are cooked through and slightly charred. Sweetcorn will take about 20 minutes to cook, onions 15-20 minutes, and fennel, tomatoes and peppers about 10 minutes.

Spanish Charcoaled Onions

SERVES 8-10

2 LARGE SPANISH OR RED ONIONS

GARLIC SALT, TO TASTE

4 TABLESPOONS DOUBLE CREAM,
HALF WHIPPED

1 TABLESPOON CRUSHED BLACK
PEPPERCORNS

25G (1OZ) BUTTER

ROSEMARY SPRIGS,
TO GARNISH

◆ Peel onions and cut into 1cm (½in) thick slices. Do not separate into rings. Season to taste with garlic salt.

◆ Brush one side with double cream and sprinkle with crushed peppercorns. Place in a tented, hinged wire basket.

◆ Barbecue over hot coals for 5-8 minutes on each side, cream side up first, until beginning to 'charcoal'. Place knobs of butter on surface of onion slices while first sides are cooking.

◆ Serve peppered side up, garnished with sprigs of rosemary.

Singed Spiced Plantains

SERVES 6-12

25G (1OZ) BUTTER, SOFTENED

2 TABLESPOONS LEMON JUICE

½ TEASPOON QUATRE ÉPICES
(SEE NOTE)

PINCH GROUND GINGER

6 PLANTAINS
(OR UNDER-RIPE BANANAS)

LEMON SLICES, TO GARNISH

Note: Quatre épices is a spicy mixture of ground pepper, cloves, nutmeg and either cinnamon or ginger. It is obtainable from many delicatessens.

◆ Mix lemon juice, quatre épices and ginger into softened butter. Set aside.

◆ Without peeling them, barbecue plantains over medium coals, turning them over until skin blackens.

◆ Slice cooked plantains in half lengthways and spoon juicy butter over the surface. Garnish with lemon slices.

Crusty Garlic Potatoes

SERVES 5-6

450G (1LB) NEW POTATOES

8 LARGE GARLIC CLOVES

2 EGGS, BEATEN

6-8 TABLESPOONS YELLOW CORNMEAL

PARSLEY SPRIGS, TO GARNISH

◆ Scrub potatoes well. Peel garlic, leaving cloves whole. Boil potatoes and garlic in salted water for 12-15 minutes until just cooked. Drain, reserving garlic.

◆ Skin potatoes as soon as they are cool enough to handle. Roughly chop garlic and, using a small skewer, insert pieces deeply into potatoes.

◆ Dip potatoes first in beaten egg and then in cornmeal. Press on well with a round-bladed knife, then dip in beaten egg once more.

◆ Barbecue potatoes on a well-oiled rack over hot coals for 10-15 minutes until crusty and golden.

◆ Serve in a basket lined with a clean napkin and garnish with parsley sprigs.

Grilled Aubergine Salad

SERVES 4

2 SMALL AUBERGINES

1 RED ONION

2 TABLESPOONS LIME JUICE

LIME SLICES AND CORIANDER LEAVES,
TO GARNISH

NAAN BREAD, TO SERVE (OPTIONAL)

MARINADE

150ML (5FL OZ) OLIVE OIL

¼ TEASPOON DRIED RED PEPPER FLAKES

½ TEASPOON CUMIN SEEDS

½ TEASPOON SESAME SEEDS

2 GARLIC CLOVES, FINELY CHOPPED

¼ TEASPOON SALT

FRESHLY GROUND BLACK PEPPER

DRESSING

150ML (5FL OZ) GREEK YOGHURT

2 TABLESPOONS FINELY CHOPPED
FRESH CORIANDER

GRATED ZEST ½ LIME

1 GARLIC CLOVE,
FINELY CHOPPED

SALT AND FRESHLY GROUND
BLACK PEPPER

◆ Cut aubergine into 1cm (½in) slices and onion into 5mm (¼in) slices. Keep onion rings in one piece by inserting 2 cocktail sticks from the outer ring to the centre. Place aubergine and onion into a large bowl.

◆ In a small bowl, combine olive oil, red pepper flakes, cumin and sesame seeds, garlic, salt and pepper. Pour mixture over aubergine and onion slices, turning to coat. Marinate for at least 30 minutes.

◆ To make dressing, mix together yoghurt, coriander, lime zest, garlic, salt and pepper. Refrigerate until required

◆ Cook vegetables on a barbecue rack over hot coals for about 5 minutes each side, until slightly blackened. Allow to cool.

◆ Remove cocktail sticks from onion slices and cut each slice in 4. Cut small aubergine slices in half and larger ones into 4.

◆ Mix onion and aubergine in a serving bowl and sprinkle with lime juice. Carefully fold in yoghurt mixture. Leave to stand at room temperature for about 1 hour to allow the flavours to develop.

◆ Garnish with lime slices and coriander leaves. Serve with warm naan bread, if desired.

Sesame-dressed Chicory

6 HEADS CHICORY, TRIMMED AND HALVED

115G (4OZ) FRENCH BEANS, TRIMMED

1 TABLESPOON SESAME SEEDS, TOASTED

DRESSING

70ML (2½ FL OZ) LIGHT OLIVE OIL

½ TEASPOON SESAME OIL

2 TEASPOONS ORANGE JUICE

1 TEASPOON BALSAMIC VINEGAR

1 TEASPOON GRATED FRESH ROOT GINGER

½ TEASPOON GRATED ORANGE ZEST

½ TEASPOON CLEAR HONEY

SALT AND FRESHLY GROUND BLACK PEPPER

◆ To prepare dressing, place olive oil, sesame oil, orange juice, balsamic vinegar, ginger, orange zest, honey, salt and pepper in a screw-top jar and shake vigorously. Leave in a cool place for the flavours to develop.

◆ Wash and dry chicory, brush with a little dressing and cook on the rack of a barbecue over hot coals for about 3 minutes on each side until leaves become lightly charred.

◆ Meanwhile, blanch beans in boiling water for 1-2 minutes until tender. Drain, refresh under cold water and pat dry.

◆ Arrange 3 chicory halves on each plate, add beans, drizzle over dressing and sprinkle with sesame seeds. Serve at once.

Spiced Squash

SERVES 4

2 SMALL BUTTERNUT SQUASH,
QUARTERED AND SEEDED

2 GARLIC CLOVES,
CRUSHED

2 TEASPOONS GROUND CUMIN

2-3 TABLESPOONS VEGETABLE OIL

JUICE ½ LIME

SALT AND FRESHLY GROUND BLACK PEPPER

◆ Using a small, sharp knife make shallow criss-cross cuts in flesh of each squash quarter.

◆ In a bowl, mix together garlic, cumin, oil and lime juice and season to taste with salt and pepper. Brush over flesh side of each piece of squash, working it well into the cuts.

◆ Cook squash quarters for 10-15 minutes until they are lightly browned and flesh is tender. Brush occasionally, while cooking, with any remaining cumin mixture.

Kebabs

Vegetable Kebabs with Coriander Sauce

2 SWEETCORN, SLICED INTO
2CM (¾IN) ROUNDS

2 RED ONIONS, CUT INTO 3-LAYER
2.5CM (1IN) PIECES

1 RED AND 1 YELLOW PEPPER, SEEDED AND
CUT INTO 2.5CM (1IN) PIECES

8 BABY PATTYPAN SQUASH, HALVED,
OR 2 SMALL COURGETTES, CUT INTO
1CM (½IN) CHUNKS

16 SMALL SHIITAKE MUSHROOMS,
STEMS REMOVED

8 FIRM CHERRY TOMATOES

85G (3OZ) BUTTER

3 TABLESPOONS OLIVE OIL

1 GARLIC CLOVE,
VERY FINELY CHOPPED

½ TEASPOON CORIANDER SEEDS,
CRUSHED

PINCH CAYENNE PEPPER

SALT AND PEPPER

CORIANDER SAUCE

85G (3OZ) FRESH CORIANDER,
TRIMMED

25G (1OZ) FLAT-LEAF PARSLEY,
TRIMMED

2 SPRING ONIONS,
CHOPPED

1 GARLIC CLOVE,
CRUSHED

2 TABLESPOONS LIME JUICE

1½ TEASPOONS TOASTED CUMIN SEEDS

¼ TEASPOON SALT

FRESHLY GROUND BLACK PEPPER, TO TASTE

85ML (3FL OZ) GREEK YOGURT

85ML (3FL OZ) DOUBLE CREAM

◆ Prepare sweetcorn, onions, peppers, pattypan squash and mushrooms and thread onto 8 skewers with cherry tomatoes. Melt butter with olive oil, garlic, coriander seeds, cayenne pepper and salt and pepper. Brush the kebabs with the melted butter mixture.

◆ To make coriander sauce, place coriander, parsley, spring onions, garlic, lime juice, cumin seeds, salt and pepper in a food processor and purée for 3 minutes, stopping to scrape the sides of the bowl frequently. Pour into a bowl and stir in yogurt and cream.

◆ Place kebabs on a barbecue. Cook for 15 minutes, turning and basting frequently, until just tender and beginning to blacken around the edges. Serve with coriander sauce.

Tofu, Leek and Mushroom Saté

350G (12OZ) PLAIN TOFU

3 LEEKS, TRIMMED

12 SHIITAKE OR BUTTON MUSHROOMS

55G (2OZ) CRUNCHY PEANUT BUTTER

25G (1OZ) CREAMED COCONUT

OLIVE OIL, FOR BRUSHING

MARINADE

2 TABLESPOONS DARK SOY SAUCE

1 GARLIC CLOVE, CRUSHED

*½ TEASPOON GRATED FRESH
ROOT GINGER*

1 SMALL RED CHILLI, SEEDED AND CHOPPED

GRATED ZEST AND JUICE 1 LIME

3 TABLESPOONS SWEET SHERRY

2 TEASPOONS CLEAR HONEY

◆ Cut tofu into 12 cubes and leeks into 12 thick slices and place in a shallow dish. Wipe mushrooms and add them to the dish.

◆ To make marinade, mix together soy sauce, garlic, ginger, chilli, lime zest and juice, sherry, honey and 3 tablespoons water. Pour over tofu mixture and marinate for several hours, stirring occasionally.

◆ To make saté sauce, place 150ml (5fl oz) of the marinade into a small pan and add peanut butter and creamed coconut. Heat gently until melted, then stir until thickened.

◆ Thread the tofu, leeks and mushrooms onto 8 bamboo skewers and brush with oil. Pour over remaining marinade and place on a barbecue for 10-12 minutes, turning and brushing with pan juices, until golden and lightly charred.

◆ Serve with sate sauce as a dip.

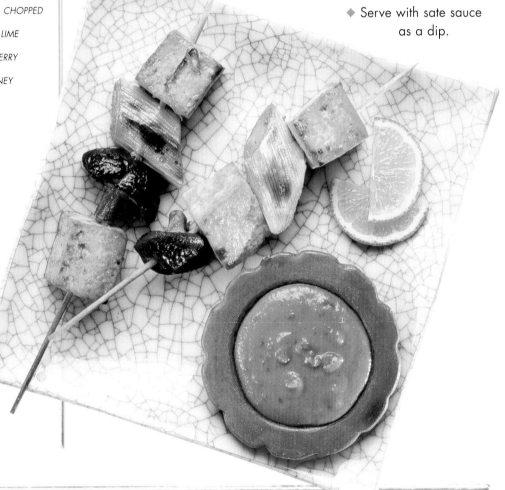

Halloumi, Courgette and Mushroom Skewers

SERVES 4

350G (12OZ) HALLOUMI CHEESE

1 RED PEPPER, HALVED, CORED AND SEEDED

1 MEDIUM COURGETTE,
CUT INTO 8 CHUNKS

8 LARGE MUSHROOMS, HALVED

115ML (4FL OZ) EXTRA VIRGIN OLIVE OIL

2 TABLESPOONS CHOPPED FRESH THYME

2 GARLIC CLOVES, CHOPPED

FRESHLY GROUND BLACK PEPPER

◆ Cut cheese and red pepper into 2.5cm (1in) squares. Place them in a shallow dish with courgette and mushrooms.

◆ In a small bowl, mix together olive oil, thyme, garlic and freshly ground black pepper and pour over vegetables. Toss gently to coat evenly.

◆ Thread cheese and vegetables on skewers, reserving any remaining oil mixture for basting. Cook on the oiled rack of a barbecue over hot coals for about 8 minutes, turning occasionally and brushing with remaining oil mixture.

◆ Skewers are ready to serve when cheese is golden and vegetables are tender.

Spicy Potato, Shallot and Fennel Kebabs

SERVES 4

24 BABY NEW POTATOES
(ABOUT 450G/1LB IN TOTAL WEIGHT)

8 SMALL SHALLOTS

16 BABY FENNEL BULBS,
(ABOUT 275G/10OZ IN TOTAL WEIGHT)

MARINADE

1 TABLESPOON MUSTARD SEEDS

1 TABLESPOON CUMIN SEEDS

1 TABLESPOON GARAM MASALA

2 TEASPOONS TURMERIC

1 TABLESPOON LEMON JUICE

115ML (4FL OZ) GROUNDNUT OIL

SALT AND FRESHLY GROUND BLACK PEPPER

◆ Cook potatoes in boiling, salted water for about 12 minutes until tender. Drain and transfer to a large mixing bowl to cool.

◆ Cook shallots in boiling water for 4 minutes, drain and, when cool enough to handle, peel them. Add to potatoes, along with fennel bulbs.

◆ To make the marinade, crush mustard and cumin seeds lightly and place them in a bowl with garam masala, turmeric, lemon juice, groundnut oil, salt and pepper. Stir to combine.

◆ Pour marinade over prepared vegetables and toss to coat well. Cover and refrigerate for 2 hours, if time permits.

◆ Remove vegetables from spicy marinade, reserving any remaining mixture for basting, and thread vegetables onto skewers.

◆ Cook kebabs on the barbecue for about 12 minutes, turning and basting with marinade while cooking.

Aubergine and Mushroom Saté

18 CHESTNUT MUSHROOMS, WIPED

1 LARGE AUBERGINE (ABOUT 350G/12OZ)

OIL, FOR BRUSHING

CHINESE LEAVES, SHREDDED, TO SERVE

½ SMALL CUCUMBER, CUT INTO MATCHSTICK STRIPS, TO SERVE

2 TABLESPOONS FINELY CHOPPED CORIANDER, TO GARNISH

MARINADE

85ML (3FL OZ) OLIVE OIL

3 TABLESPOONS SOY SAUCE

1 TABLESPOON WINE VINEGAR

1 GARLIC CLOVE, CRUSHED

SALT AND FRESHLY GROUND BLACK PEPPER

SATE SAUCE

115G (4OZ) FRESH PEANUTS, ROASTED

2 TEASPOONS CORIANDER SEEDS, ROASTED

2 TEASPOONS VEGETABLE OIL

2 GARLIC CLOVES, FINELY CHOPPED

1 SHALLOT OR ½ SMALL ONION, FINELY CHOPPED

2 TEASPOONS FINELY CHOPPED LEMON GRASS (OR ½ TEASPOON DRIED)

½ TEASPOON CHILLI POWDER

1 TEASPOON GROUND CUMIN SEEDS

1 TEASPOON INDONESIAN SOY SAUCE

1 TEASPOON DARK SOFT BROWN SUGAR

½ TEASPOON SALT

JUICE ½ LIME OR LEMON

2 TABLESPOONS NATURAL YOGHURT

FRESHLY GROUND BLACK PEPPER

◆ Cut mushrooms in half. Cut aubergine into 2cm (¾in) slices then cut each slice into 4 segments. Place vegetables in a shallow dish.

◆ To make the marinade, in a small bowl, mix together olive oil, soy sauce, wine vinegar, garlic, salt and pepper.

◆ Spoon marinade over vegetables, making sure they are thoroughly coated. Leave for at least 1 hour, turning occasionally.

◆ To make saté sauce, place peanuts and coriander seeds in a coffee grinder or blender and grind as finely as possible.

◆ Heat oil in a saucepan. Add garlic, shallot or onion, lemon grass, chilli powder and cumin seeds and stir-fry for about 1 minute until lightly browned.

◆ Add 450ml (¾ pint) water, soy sauce, dark soft brown sugar, salt and peanut mixture. Bring to the boil, stirring. Reduce heat and simmer for 15-20 minutes until thickened, stirring frequently.

◆ Allow to cool slightly, then stir in lime or lemon juice, yoghurt and black pepper.

◆ Thread pieces of mushroom and aubergine alternately onto 12 skewers. Brush with oil and place on a barbecue rack over hot coals for about 10 minutes, turning frequently and brushing with oil, until browned.

◆ Place on a bed of Chinese leaves and cucumber strips. Spoon over some of the saté sauce and serve the rest in a bowl. Sprinkle with coriander and serve immediately.

Skewered New Potatoes

SERVES 6

*32 BABY NEW POTATOES
(ABOUT 700G/1½LB IN TOTAL WEIGHT)*

4 TABLESPOONS OLIVE OIL

*SEA SALT AND
FRESHLY GROUND BLACK PEPPER*

HERB BUTTER

*85G (3OZ) BUTTER,
SOFTENED*

*2 TABLESPOONS CHOPPED FRESH HERBS
OF YOUR CHOICE*

SALT AND FRESHLY GROUND BLACK PEPPER

◆ Scrub potatoes and cook them in boiling, salted water for about 12 minutes or until tender. Drain potatoes and, while they are still warm, toss with olive oil and plenty of salt and freshly ground black pepper. Thread 4 potatoes onto each of 8 skewers and set aside until required.

◆ To make herb butter, in a bowl, mix together butter, chopped herbs, salt and pepper. Roll butter into a sausage shape on a piece of greaseproof paper or plastic wrap. Refrigerate butter until it becomes firm enough to slice.

◆ Cook potatoes on a rack over hot coals for 12-15 minutes, turning them frequently. Serve hot with herb butter.

Patty Pan, Onion and Aubergine Kebabs

SERVES 4

16 SMALL PATTYPAN SQUASH

8 BABY AUBERGINES, HALVED LENGTHWAYS

8 BABY ONIONS, UNPEELED

MARINADE

4 TABLESPOONS CHOPPED FRESH CORIANDER

115ML (4FL OZ) OLIVE OIL

1 TEASPOON GARAM MASALA

1 TEASPOON DRIED CHILLI FLAKES

2 GARLIC CLOVES, CRUSHED

SALT AND FRESHLY GROUND BLACK PEPPER

◆ To make marinade, mix together in a large bowl chopped coriander, olive oil, garam masala, dried chilli flakes, garlic, salt and pepper.

◆ Boil pattypan squash for 4 minutes, drain and add to marinade, along with aubergines.

◆ Boil onions for 5 minutes, then drain, peel and halve them. Add onions to bowl of vegetables. Toss gently to coat evenly with marinade. Cover and refrigerate for 2 hours.

◆ Thread marinated vegetables onto skewers, reserving marinade for basting. Cook kebabs on a prepared barbecue for about 10 minutes, turning and basting occasionally while cooking.

Oriental Tofu Skewers

SERVES 4

250G (9OZ) TOFU, CUT INTO 16 CUBES

1 LARGE ORANGE PEPPER

8 CHERRY TOMATOES

85G (3OZ) BROCCOLI,
DIVIDED INTO 8 FLORETS

SESAME MARINADE

3 TABLESPOONS VEGETABLE OIL

1 TABLESPOON SESAME OIL

1 TABLESPOON SOY SAUCE

1 TEASPOON GRATED FRESH ROOT GINGER

1 TEASPOON SESAME SEEDS

2 TABLESPOONS RICE WINE VINEGAR

1 SPRING ONION, FINELY CHOPPED

◆ To make marinade, mix together in a large bowl vegetable oil, sesame oil, soy sauce, ginger, sesame seeds, rice wine vinegar and spring onion.

◆ Add tofu cubes to marinade, toss gently to coat, cover and refrigerate for 2 hours.

◆ Place pepper on a rack over hot coals and barbecue, turning frequently until skin blisters and becomes charred.

◆ Place pepper in a plastic bag and leave to cool and soften for 30 minutes. Peel and discard skin and seeds. Cut flesh into 8 thick slices.

◆ Remove tofu from marinade, reserving remaining marinade for basting. Thread tofu, pepper strips, tomatoes and broccoli on skewers.

◆ Cook skewers on the barbecue for 8-10 minutes, turning and basting them while cooking. Just before serving, pour any remaining marinade over tofu skewers.

Mushroom and Mozzarella Brochettes

16 FRESH SHIITAKE MUSHROOMS,
(ABOUT 115G/4OZ IN TOTAL WEIGHT)

16 BUTTON MUSHROOMS,
(ABOUT 225G/8OZ IN TOTAL WEIGHT)

16 MINI MOZZARELLA CHEESE BALLS

MARINADE

ZEST AND JUICE
2 SMALL LEMONS

2 TABLESPOONS OLIVE OIL

2 TEASPOONS CHILLI OIL

3 TABLESPOONS CHOPPED
FRESH ROSEMARY

½ SMALL FRESH RED CHILLI,
SEEDED AND FINELY CHOPPED

½ SMALL FRESH GREEN CHILLI,
SEEDED AND FINELY CHOPPED

2 GARLIC CLOVES, CRUSHED

SALT AND FRESHLY GROUND BLACK PEPPER

◆ To make marinade, mix together in a small bowl lemon zest and juice, olive and chilli oils, rosemary, red and green chillies, garlic, salt and freshly ground black pepper.

◆ Place two types of mushrooms and mini mozzarella balls in a mixing bowl. Pour over marinade and toss gently to coat evenly. Cover and refrigerate for 2 hours.

◆ Remove marinated mushrooms and cheese from the dish, reserving any remaining marinade for basting, and thread mushrooms and cheese onto skewers. Cook brochettes on a prepared medium-hot barbecue for about 10 minutes, turning and basting them while cooking.

Note: These kebabs taste even better if cooked on rosemary branches rather than on conventional metal skewers.

Hot Hot Aloo

24 BABY NEW POTATOES
(ABOUT 450G/1LB IN TOTAL WEIGHT)

4 TABLESPOONS LIME PICKLE

4 TABLESPOONS OLIVE OIL

2 TEASPOONS TOMATO PURÉE

2 TEASPOONS GROUND CARDAMOM

2 TABLESPOONS NATURAL YOGHURT

LIME SLICES, TO GARNISH

◆ Wash and scrub potatoes. Cook in salted water until tender but firm. Drain and leave to go cold. Thread onto 4-6 skewers.

◆ Place lime pickle in a bowl and, using kitchen scissors, cut up any large pieces of pickle. Blend in oil, tomato purée, cardamom and yoghurt. Spoon mixture over skewered potatoes so that each potato is well coated.

◆ Barbecue potatoes on rack over hot coals for about 10 minutes, turning frequently.

◆ Garnish with lime slices and serve immediately.

Mixed Vegetable Kebabs

*1 LARGE AUBERGINE
(ABOUT 350G/ 12OZ),
CUT INTO BITE-SIZED PIECES*

*½ LARGE RED PEPPER,
SEEDED AND CUT INTO 2CM (¾IN) CUBES*

*½ LARGE YELLOW PEPPER,
SEEDED AND CUT INTO 2CM (¾IN) CUBES*

*4 SMALL COURGETTES, TRIMMED AND CUT
INTO 1CM (½IN) SLICES*

8 SHALLOTS, QUARTERED

16 BUTTON MUSHROOMS

16 CHERRY TOMATOES

*OREGANO AND PARSLEY SPRIGS,
TO GARNISH*

MARINADE

85ML (3FL OZ) OLIVE OIL

1 TABLESPOON RASPBERRY VINEGAR

½ TEASPOON SALT

*½ TEASPOON FRESHLY GROUND
BLACK PEPPER*

1 TEASPOON DRY MUSTARD

1 TABLESPOON LIGHT SOFT BROWN SUGAR

*1 TABLESPOON CHOPPED
FRESH OREGANO*

*1 TABLESPOON CHOPPED
FRESH PARSLEY*

◆ To make marinade, mix together in a bowl olive oil, raspberry vinegar, salt, pepper, mustard, light soft brown sugar, oregano and parsley, stirring until well blended.

◆ Place aubergine in a colander or sieve over a bowl, sprinkle with salt, cover with a plate, weight the top and leave for 30 minutes. Rinse aubergine thoroughly to remove salt, then press out water.

◆ Add aubergine, red and yellow pepper, courgettes, shallots, mushrooms and tomatoes to marinade and turn vegetables carefully to coat completely. Cover with plastic wrap and leave to marinate in the refrigerator for 1 hour.

◆ Thread a mixture of vegetables onto skewers. Cook on the rack of the barbecue over hot coals for 3-5 minutes, brushing with marinade until just tender.

◆ Arrange on a serving dish, garnished with oregano and parsley sprigs.

Main Meals

Chicory and Tomato Gratin

4 LARGE PLUMP HEADS CHICORY,
HALVED LENGTHWAYS

SALT AND FRESHLY GROUND BLACK PEPPER

OLIVE OIL, FOR BRUSHING

2 GARLIC CLOVES, FINELY CHOPPED

200G (7OZ) CAN CHOPPED TOMATOES

2 TEASPOONS FINELY CHOPPED
FRESH MARJORAM OR BASIL

45G (1½OZ) DRY BREADCRUMBS

45G (1½OZ) FRESHLY GRATED
VEGETARIAN PARMESAN

55G (2OZ) BUTTER

◆ Make 2 or 3 deep cuts in the base of chicory heads. With cut side down, place on the rack over hot coals for 3-5 minutes until just beginning to blacken.

◆ Turn over, sprinkle with salt and freshly ground black pepper and brush generously with olive oil, working oil between leaves.

◆ Cook on the barbecue, cut side upwards, for 10-15 minutes until just tender. Transfer chicory to a shallow dish.

◆ Meanwhile, heat 1 tablespoon of olive oil in a small saucepan. Add garlic and gently fry for 30 seconds, then add tomatoes and marjoram or basil. Season to taste with salt and freshly ground black pepper. Simmer for 5 minutes, stirring occasionally, then pour mixture over chicory.

◆ Combine breadcrumbs and Parmesan cheese, then sprinkle it over chicory. Dot with butter.

◆ Wrap each chicory half tightly in a piece of aluminium foil and place on the barbecue rack over hot coals. Cook for about 10 minutes, turning half way through cooking time.

Noodles with Marinated Vegetables

SERVES 4

2 SMALL RED ONIONS, UNPEELED

2 HEADS PURPLE 'WET' GARLIC

4 SMALL COURGETTES

2 SMALL PLUMP HEADS CHICORY

1 AUBERGINE

1 LARGE YELLOW PEPPER, SEEDED

OLIVE OIL, FOR BRUSHING

115G (4OZ) EGG VERMICELLI

MARINADE

HANDFUL TORN BASIL LEAVES

HANDFUL FENNEL FRONDS

HANDFUL CORIANDER,
TRIMMED AND ROUGHLY CHOPPED

2.5CM (1IN) PIECE FRESH ROOT GINGER,
FINELY CHOPPED

2 LARGE GARLIC CLOVES,
CHOPPED

1 FRESH CHILLI,
SEEDED AND CHOPPED

FINELY GRATED ZEST AND
JUICE 1 LIME

115ML (4FL OZ) OLIVE OIL

55G (2OZ) PEANUTS,
TOASTED

1 TEASPOON
MUSCOVADO SUGAR

½ TEASPOON SALT

◆ To make marinade, place basil, fennel fronds, coriander, ginger, garlic, chilli, lime zest and juice, olive oil, peanuts, sugar and salt in a blender or food processor and purée until smooth.

◆ Cut red onions and garlic in half crossways and courgettes and chicory lengthways. Place vegetables in a single layer in a dish.

◆ Brush vegetables with marinade and drizzle with olive oil. Cover and refrigerate for at least 2 hours, preferably overnight.

◆ Remove vegetables, scraping off and reserving marinade, and place on a rack over medium-hot coals. Grill for 10-15 minutes, brushing with oil and turning occasionally, until tender and beginning to blacken.

◆ Meanwhile, cook vermicelli, following packaging instructions. Drain, return to the pan and toss with reserved marinade.

◆ Arrange a nest of vermicelli on 4 plates and top with a selection of grilled vegetables.

Savoy Cabbage Parcels

SERVES 4

4 LARGE SAVOY OR POINTED GREEN CABBAGE LEAVES

85G (3OZ) BUTTER

115G (4OZ) LEEKS, THINLY SLICED

1 LARGE CARROT, PEELED AND COARSELY GRATED

175G (6OZ) COOKED BROWN BASMATI RICE

25G (1OZ) PUMPKIN SEEDS, LIGHTLY TOASTED

2 TABLESPOONS CHOPPED FRESH TARRAGON

SALT AND FRESHLY GROUND BLACK PEPPER

◆ Cut away tough stalks from cabbage leaves, then blanch leaves in boiling, salted water for 1-2 minutes until they are just tender. Drain and refresh in cold water, then lay cabbage leaves on paper towels to dry .

◆ Melt 55g (2oz) of butter in a pan, add leeks and sauté them for 3 minutes. Stir in carrot and sauté for a further minute. Remove pan from heat and stir in rice, pumpkin seeds, tarragon and seasoning.

◆ Lay a cabbage leaf on a large piece of aluminium foil and place one quarter of rice mixture in the centre. Fold cabbage around filling to form a parcel, dot with one quarter of remaining butter and fold up foil to enclose cabbage. Repeat with remaining cabbage leaves and filling.

◆ Cook foil parcels on a prepared barbecue for 13-15 minutes, until cabbage is tender and filling is heated through.

Peppers Stuffed with Nutty Rice

SERVES 4

225G (8OZ) BASMATI RICE

1 TEASPOON SAFFRON STRANDS

4 TABLESPOONS VEGETABLE OIL

1 RED ONION, THINLY SLICED

4 SMALL GARLIC CLOVES, CRUSHED

55G (2OZ) PINE NUTS, TOASTED

25G (1OZ) PISTACHIO NUTS, CHOPPED

4 TABLESPOONS CHOPPED FRESH PARSLEY

SALT AND FRESHLY GROUND BLACK PEPPER

4 MEDIUM RED PEPPERS

OIL, FOR BRUSHING

◆ Infuse saffron threads in 3 tablespoons boiling water for 10 minutes.

◆ Add saffron and its water to a saucepan of boiling, salted water with basmati rice. Bring back to the boil and cook for 10 minutes. Drain rice and place in a mixing bowl.

◆ Heat oil in a pan and sauté onion and garlic for 2-3 minutes. Add to rice, with pine nuts, pistachios, parsley and seasoning. Toss to combine.

◆ Halve peppers lengthways and core and seed, leaving stalks intact. Divide nutty rice between pepper halves.

◆ Lightly oil 4 large pieces of aluminium foil and place 2 pepper halves on each piece of foil. Fold foil over to enclose fillings.

◆ Cook on a prepared barbecue for about 20 minutes, until peppers are tender and rice is hot.

Grilled Vegetable Pizza

SERVES 4

225G (8OZ) STRONG PLAIN FLOUR

½ TEASPOON FAST-ACTION DRIED YEAST

½ TEASPOON SALT

100ML (3½FL OZ) WARMED WATER

1 TABLESPOON OLIVE OIL

TOPPING

1 RED PEPPER, QUARTERED AND SEEDED

1 SMALL COURGETTE, SLICED

1 SMALL AUBERGINE, SLICED

1 SMALL ONION, THINLY SLICED

6 LARGE RIPE TOMATOES, HALVED AND SEEDED

2 TABLESPOONS PESTO SAUCE

SALT AND FRESHLY GROUND BLACK PEPPER

150G (5OZ) MOZZARELLA CHEESE, GRATED

◆ In a bowl, mix together flour, yeast and salt. Make a well in the centre and work in the water and oil to form a stiff dough. Knead for 5 minutes, place in an oiled bowl, cover and leave to rise in a warm place for 30 minutes until doubled in size.

◆ Preheat oven to 230°C/450°F/gas mark 8 and place a pizza plate or baking sheet on the top shelf.

◆ Brush peppers, courgette, aubergine and onion slices with a little oil and place on the rack of a barbecue over hot coals until charred all over.

◆ Place tomato halves skin side up on the barbecue rack and cook until blistered. Peel and discard skin and mash flesh with pesto sauce and salt and pepper.

◆ Roll out dough to a 23-25cm (9-10in) round. Spread tomato mixture over pizza round and arrange barbecued vegetables over the top. Sprinkle over cheese and transfer to pizza plate or baking sheet.

◆ Bake pizza for 25-30 minutes until bubbling and golden.

Falafel Patties with Yoghurt and Mint Dip

SERVES 4

SERVES 4

2 TABLESPOONS VEGETABLE OIL

1 TEASPOON CUMIN SEEDS

1 ONION, FINELY CHOPPED

2 GARLIC CLOVES, CRUSHED

1 TEASPOON CHOPPED
FRESH GREEN CHILLI

½ TEASPOON TURMERIC

432G (15OZ) CAN CHICKPEAS,
DRAINED

SALT AND FRESHLY GROUND
BLACK PEPPER

55G (2OZ) FRESH WHITE
BREADCRUMBS

1 EGG, BEATEN

2 TABLESPOONS CHOPPED
FRESH CORIANDER

FLOUR, FOR COATING

OIL, FOR BRUSHING

LEMON WEDGES, TO SERVE

PITTA BREAD, TO SERVE

YOGHURT AND MINT DIP

115ML (4FL OZ) GREEK YOGHURT

4 TABLESPOONS CHOPPED
FRESH MINT

1 TEASPOON LEMON JUICE

PINCH GROUND CUMIN

SALT AND FRESHLY GROUND
BLACK PEPPER

◆ To make dip, in a bowl, mix together yoghurt, mint, lemon juice, cumin and seasoning. Cover and refrigerate until required.

◆ Heat vegetable oil in a frying pan, add cumin seeds, onion and garlic and sauté for 5 minutes. Add chopped chilli and turmeric and cook for a further 2 minutes.

◆ Transfer spice mixture to a blender or food processor, add chickpeas and seasoning, and blend or process briefly until chickpeas are roughly mashed and combined with spices.

◆ Transfer to a bowl and add breadcrumbs, beaten egg and coriander. Mix to combine and divide into 8 portions. With floured hands, shape into patties and refrigerate these falafel for about 4 hours.

◆ Brush falafel all over with oil. Place on an oiled griddle plate, or in a wire basket, and cook on the barbecue 6-7 minutes on each side.

◆ Serve hot with dip, lemon wedges and pitta bread.

Aubergine Layers

SERVES 6

2 LARGE AUBERGINES

1 TEASPOON SALT

2 RED PEPPERS

70ML (2½FL OZ) OLIVE OIL

*300G (10OZ) MOZZARELLA CHEESE,
THINLY SLICED*

OREGANO LEAVES, TO GARNISH

TOMATO SAUCE

2 TABLESPOONS OLIVE OIL

2 GARLIC CLOVES, CRUSHED

*700G (1½LB) PLUM TOMATOES, PEELED,
SEEDED AND CHOPPED (SEE NOTE)*

2 TEASPOONS CHOPPED FRESH OREGANO

SALT AND FRESHLY GROUND BLACK PEPPER

◆ Cut aubergines into 1cm (½in) thick slices. Place in a colander, sprinkle with salt and leave for 1 hour.

◆ Place peppers on the rack of a barbecue over hot coals until skins are beginning to blacken. Place into a plastic bag for a few minutes while still hot. Remove from plastic bag, peel and cut into thin strips.

◆ To make tomato sauce, heat olive oil in a saucepan. Add garlic and cook, stirring, for a few minutes until soft. Add tomatoes, oregano, salt and pepper and cook gently, stirring, for 2 minutes, without allowing tomatoes to lose their texture. Remove from heat and keep warm.

◆ Rinse aubergines well, drain and dry thoroughly with paper towels. Brush with 55ml (2fl oz) of the olive oil, place on barbecue rack and cook on both sides until soft and beginning to brown.

◆ Place half the aubergine slices onto a baking sheet or plate. Arrange mozzarella slices on top, cutting to fit if necessary. Top with half the pepper strips. Place remaining aubergine slices on top. Drizzle over remaining olive oil.

◆ Place in a hinged wire basket and barbecue over hot coals for about 2 minutes on each side until heated through, but do not allow mozzarella to melt.

◆ Remove from the wire basket onto serving plates, arrange remaining strips of pepper on top, garnish with oregano leaves and serve with tomato sauce.

Note: To peel tomatoes, make slits in the skin, place in boiling water for a minute or two, refresh in cold water, then peel away skins.

Stuffed Aubergines

*6 SMALL AUBERGINES,
EACH ABOUT 185G (6OZ)*

25G (1OZ) BUTTER

1 ONION, FINELY CHOPPED

1 GARLIC CLOVE, CRUSHED

225G (8OZ) CAN CHOPPED TOMATOES

85G (3OZ) FRESH BREADCRUMBS

*55G (2OZ) GRATED VEGETARIAN
CHEDDAR CHEESE*

1 TEASPOON DRIED OREGANO

SALT AND FRESHLY GROUND BLACK PEPPER

OREGANO SPRIGS, TO GARNISH

◆ Cut off a thin slice along the length of each aubergine and reserve. Scoop out flesh from aubergines, leaving a 0.5cm (¼in) wall. Finely chop reserved flesh.

◆ Melt butter in a saucepan and gently fry onion and garlic until soft. Add chopped aubergine and continue frying until tender.

◆ Remove from heat and stir in tomatoes, breadcrumbs, cheese and oregano. Season to taste with salt and freshly ground black pepper.

◆ Pack filling into aubergine shells. Replace lids and wrap separately in squares of lightly oiled, double-thickness aluminium foil.

◆ Barbecue on rack over medium coals, or cook directly in coals, for 20-30 minutes.

◆ Garnish with sprigs of oregano and serve.

Potato and Egg Peppers

SERVES 4

4 SMALL GREEN PEPPERS

*4 HARD-BOILED EGGS,
SHELLED*

225G (8OZ) COOKED POTATO

3 TABLESPOONS MAYONNAISE

2 TEASPOONS FRENCH MUSTARD

*1 ROUNDED TABLESPOON CHOPPED
FRESH CHIVES*

1 TEASPOON PAPRIKA

½ TEASPOON GARLIC SALT

FRESHLY GROUND BLACK PEPPER

*PARSLEY SPRIGS,
TO GARNISH*

◆ Cut away a thin slice from stalk end of each pepper. Remove core, seeds and pith.

◆ Coarsely chop hard-boiled eggs and potato and place in a mixing bowl. Add mayonnaise, mustard, chives, paprika, garlic salt and black pepper to taste. Mix well. Carefully spoon mixture into green peppers.

◆ Wrap each pepper separately in lightly buttered, double-thickness aluminium foil and barbecue on rack, or directly in coals, for about 30 minutes until peppers are tender, turning packets over occasionally. Garnish with sprigs of parsley.

Brazil Nut Burgers

SERVES 6

45G (1½OZ) BUTTER

1 ONION, FINELY CHOPPED

1 CELERY STICK, FINELY CHOPPED

½ SMALL GREEN PEPPER, SEEDED AND CHOPPED

225G (8OZ) SHELLED BRAZIL NUTS, GROUND

1 CARROT, GRATED

1 TEASPOON YEAST EXTRACT

300ML (10FL OZ) VEGETABLE STOCK

55G (2OZ) BULGAR (CRACKED WHEAT)

SALT AND FRESHLY GROUND BLACK PEPPER

2 EGGS, BEATEN

FLOUR, FOR DUSTING

½ SMALL GREEN PEPPER, SLICED INTO 6 RINGS, TO GARNISH

◆ In a heavy-based saucepan, melt butter and gently fry onion, celery and green pepper until soft. Stir in nuts and cook for 3-4 minutes, stirring continually to bring out the flavour.

◆ Stir grated carrot, yeast extract and vegetable stock into mixture and bring to boil, then simmer for 5 minutes. Mix in bulgar wheat and season to taste with salt and freshly ground black pepper. Leave mixture to cool.

◆ Bind together with beaten eggs to the consistency of thick paste. Shape mixture into 6 burgers and dust with flour. Place burgers on a well-oiled griddle pan

◆ Place on rack and cook over hot coals for 10 minutes, turning burgers once during cooking. Carefully remove burgers from grill and garnish with green pepper rings.

Green Lentil Courgettes

SERVES 4

3 LARGE FIRM COURGETTES

2 SPRING ONIONS, FINELY CHOPPED

1 SMALL GREEN PEPPER, FINELY CHOPPED

1 TOMATO, PEELED AND CHOPPED

115G (4OZ) COOKED GREEN LENTILS

1 TEASPOON FRESH BASIL LEAVES, CHOPPED

SALT AND FRESHLY GROUND BLACK PEPPER

3 TABLESPOONS GRATED, ROASTED HAZELNUTS

BASIL SPRIGS, TO GARNISH

◆ Halve courgettes lengthwise. Scoop pulp into a bowl, leaving 0.5-cm (¼-in) thick shells to prevent courgettes from collapsing. Reserve shells.

◆ Add spring onion, green pepper and tomato to courgette pulp and mix in lentils and basil. Season to taste. Pile mixture high into reserved shells.

◆ Place courgette halves individually onto large squares of double-thickness aluminium foil. Wrap up securely, leaving a space above stuffing for steam to circulate.

◆ Barbecue on rack over hot coals for about 20 minutes until courgettes are tender but firm. Open packets and sprinkle hazelnuts over stuffing. Garnish with sprigs of basil to serve.

Grilled Tomato and Asparagus Salad

SERVES 4

12 THICK ASPARAGUS SPEARS, TRIMMED

EXTRA VIRGIN OLIVE OIL, FOR BRUSHING

8 RIPE PLUM TOMATOES,
QUARTERED AND SEEDED

55G (2OZ) BABY SPINACH LEAVES

175G (6OZ) MOZZARELLA CHEESE, SLICED

8 BLACK OLIVES

4 TABLESPOONS PESTO

EXTRA VIRGIN OLIVE OIL, FOR DRESSING

◆ Slice asparagus spears in half and brush with a little oil. Place in a wire basket, or directly onto the barbecue rack, and cook for about 6 minutes, turning frequently, until charred and tender. Leave to cool.

◆ Drizzle a little oil over tomato quarters and barbecue for 2-3 minutes until just softened. Leave to cool, then peel away and discard skins.

◆ Arrange asparagus and tomatoes on plates. Add spinach leaves, mozzarella slices and olives.

◆ Mix pesto with extra virgin olive oil to make a dressing and drizzle over salad. Serve immediately.

Stuffed Onions with Sun-dried Tomatoes

SERVES 2

3 LARGE ONIONS, UNPEELED

*115G (4OZ) SUN-DRIED TOMATOES IN OIL,
DRAINED AND THINLY SLICED*

115G (4OZ) GOAT'S CHEESE, CUBED

1 GARLIC CLOVE, CRUSHED

55G (2OZ) FRESH WHITE BREADCRUMBS

25G (1OZ) PINE NUTS, TOASTED

1 TABLESPOON CHOPPED FRESH BASIL

1 TEASPOON CHOPPED FRESH THYME

1 EGG

SALT AND FRESHLY GROUND BLACK PEPPER

CREME FRAICHE, TO SERVE (OPTIONAL)

◆ Place unpeeled onions in a large pan and cover with cold water. Bring to the boil and cook for 15 minutes, until tender. Drain onions and cool.

◆ Place tomatoes, cheese, garlic, breadcrumbs, pine nuts, basil and thyme in a large bowl and mix together.

◆ Cut cooled onions in half, through the root and tip, and carefully cut out most of the flesh, leaving 1 or 2 layers to keep the shape and form the empty shells.

◆ Discard half the flesh, finely chop the rest and stir into the reserved filling. Lightly beat egg and stir into filling.

◆ Place each onion half on a large square of double-thickness aluminium foil. Spoon filling into empty shells, packing mixture in well. Fold foil over filling and secure.

◆ Cook on the barbecue rack over hot coals for about 20-25 minutes, or directly in the coals for about 15 minutes.

◆ Serve hot or cold, with crème fraîche if desired.

Note: This dish also makes an ideal starter, in which case it will serve 6.

Fruit

Kiwis and Stem Ginger

6 FIRM KIWI FRUIT, UNPEELED

5-6 TABLESPOONS STEM GINGER SYRUP

150ML (5FL OZ) WHIPPING CREAM

1 TABLESPOON ICING SUGAR

*6 PIECES STEM GINGER,
CUT IN HALF LENGTHWAYS*

*1 TABLESPOON CHOPPED SHELLED
PISTACHIO NUTS*

◆ Rinse and dry kiwi fruit and halve lengthways. Remove firm cores, chop and reserve. Spoon a little ginger syrup over kiwi flesh and pierce with a skewer to help absorption.

◆ Stiffly whip cream with icing sugar and refrigerate until required.

◆ Place pieces of stem ginger in cavities in kiwi fruit. Place filled kiwi halves, skin sides down, onto squares of aluminium foil and pour a little more ginger syrup over ginger. Wrap up securely.

◆ Barbecue over medium hot coals for 10-15 minutes, turning parcels over towards end of cooking time.

◆ Open parcels and sprinkle cut surfaces of fruit with nuts and reserved chopped cores. Serve with sweetened whipped cream.

Spiced Fruit Kebabs

*1KG (2¼LB) PREPARED MIXED FRUITS,
SUCH AS MANGO, PAPAYA, PINEAPPLE,
NECTARINE, PLUM, BANANA, LYCHEES,
CHERRIES*

150G (5OZ) UNSALTED BUTTER

*3 TABLESPOONS GRATED FRESH
ROOT GINGER*

1 TABLESPOON ICING SUGAR

1 TABLESPOON LIME JUICE

◆ Soak about 20 bamboo skewers in water for 30 minutes.

◆ Cut fruit into bite-sized chunks. Thread a selection of pieces of fruit onto each skewer.

◆ Melt butter and stir in fresh root ginger, icing sugar and lime juice. Brush over kebabs.

◆ Cook kebabs on the barbecue, over medium coals, turning frequently and brushing with butter mixture, for about 5 minutes, until beginning to caramelise.

Baked Demelza Apples

SERVES 4

25G (1OZ) RAISINS

25G (1OZ) SULTANAS

*5 TABLESPOONS GINGER WINE,
MADEIRA OR SWEET SHERRY*

85G (3OZ) FLAKED ALMONDS, TOASTED

1-2 TABLESPOONS MARMALADE

4 LARGE COOKING APPLES

*CHILLED WHIPPED CREAM,
TO SERVE*

◆ Place raisins and sultanas into a small bowl and add ginger wine, Madeira or sherry. Leave to soak for several hours.

◆ Drain dried fruit, reserving liquid, and place in a bowl. Add flaked almonds and marmalade and stir to combine.

◆ Wash and dry apples, but do not peel. Remove core using an apple corer and score a line around each apple. Stand each apple on a piece of double-thickness aluminium foil.

◆ Fill apple cavities with dried fruit mixture, pushing it down firmly. Fold up edges of foil, leaving a gap at the top, and pour strained liquid over apples.

◆ Place apple parcels on the barbecue rack over medium coals for 45-50 minutes, turning occasionally, until soft. Alternatively, cook directly in the coals for 20-30 minutes.

◆ Remove apples from the foil, place on serving dishes, and pile a spoonful of whipped cream on top of each apple to serve.

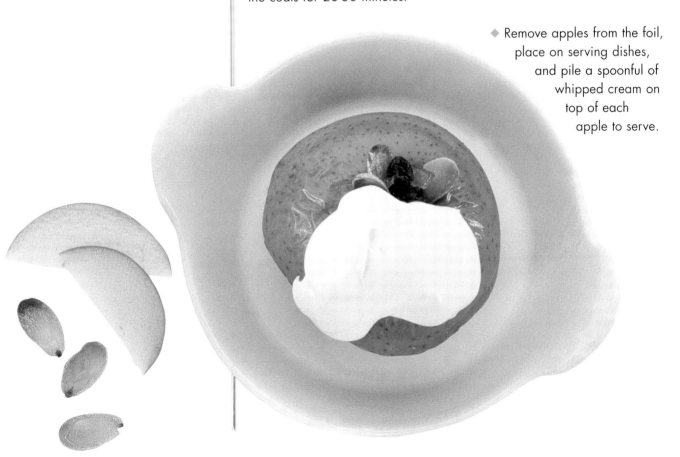

Caribbean Fruit Kebabs with Honey Glaze

SERVES 6

*1 SMALL MANGO,
PEELED AND STONED*

*½ SMALL PINEAPPLE, CUT
LENGTHWAYS AND PEELED*

2 SMALL DESERT APPLES

*2 LARGE BANANAS,
PEELED*

24 KUMQUATS

GLAZE

150ML (5FL OZ) CLEAR HONEY

ZEST AND JUICE 1 ORANGE

¼ TEASPOON GROUND CLOVES

◆ Cut mango flesh into 12 chunks. Halve pineapple, remove centre core, and cut each quarter into 6 slices. Cut apples into 12 wedges, cut bananas into 12 thick slices and wash and dry kumquats.

◆ Thread 2 kumquats and 1 piece each of the other prepared fruits onto each of 12 skewers. Place in a large shallow dish.

◆ To make the glaze, blend together honey, orange zest and juice and ground cloves and pour over kebabs. Cover and marinate for 30 minutes, turning once.

◆ Cook kebabs on the barbecue over hot coals for 6-8 minutes, turning and basting frequently with glaze, until fruit is browned and sizzling. Serve hot.

Foiled Rum Bananas

SERVES 6

6 BANANAS, PEELED

2 TABLESPOONS CHOPPED STEM GINGER

2 TABLESPOONS STEM GINGER SYRUP

4 TABLESPOONS DARK RUM

2 TABLESPOONS ORANGE JUICE

25G (1OZ) UNSALTED BUTTER

*CREAM OR NATURAL YOGHURT,
TO SERVE*

◆ Cut each banana in half lengthways and place in the centre of a double layer of aluminium foil. Pull edges up, leaving a small gap at the top.

◆ Add 1 teaspoon chopped stem ginger, 1 teaspoon syrup, 2 teaspoons rum, 1 teaspoon orange juice and a knob of butter to each parcel.

◆ Turn edges of foil over to seal well and cook on the barbecue over hot coals for 5-6 minutes until bananas are succulent and tender.

◆ Serve immediately with a little cream or yoghurt.

Figs with Cinnamon Cream

SERVES 6

9 LARGE RIPE FIGS

55G (2OZ) UNSALTED BUTTER

4 TEASPOONS BRANDY

3 TEASPOONS BROWN SUGAR

FLAKED ALMONDS, TO DECORATE

CINNAMON CREAM

150ML (5FL OZ) DOUBLE CREAM

1 TEASPOON GROUND CINNAMON

1 TABLESPOON BRANDY

2 TEASPOONS CLEAR HONEY

◆ To make cinnamon cream, in a small bowl, combine cream, ground cinnamon, brandy and honey. Cover and refrigerate for 30 minutes to allow flavours to develop.

◆ Halve figs and thread onto 6 skewers. Melt butter in a small pan and stir in brandy. Brush figs with brandy butter and sprinkle with a little sugar.

◆ Place kebabs on the barbecue over medium coals for 4-5 minutes until bubbling and golden.

◆ Whip cinnamon cream until just holding its shape and serve with grilled figs, decorated with flaked almonds.

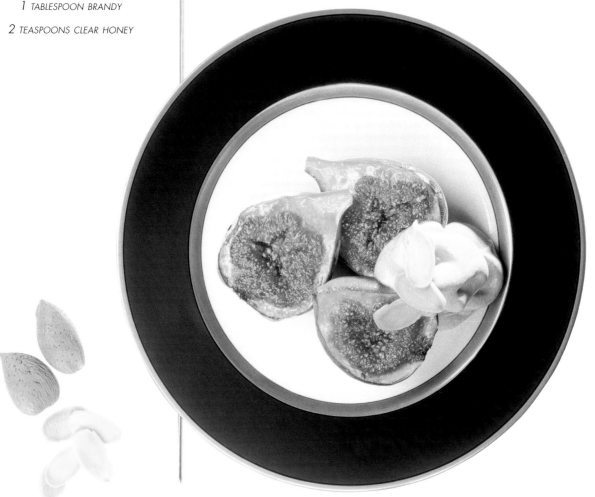

Hot Tropicanas

SERVES 6

3 PINK GRAPEFRUIT

8 LYCHEES

2 KUMQUATS,
RINSED AND DRIED

1 GUAVA

1 PAW PAW

1 SMALL MANGO

4 TABLESPOONS GOLDEN SYRUP

25G (1OZ) BUTTER

2 TABLESPOONS DESICCATED
COCONUT, TOASTED
(SEE BELOW)

MINT SPRIGS,
TO GARNISH

◆ Halve grapefruit, separate and remove segments to a large mixing bowl and drain shells. Scrape out grapefruit shells, discarding membranes.

◆ Peel and stone lychees. Slice kumquats. Halve guava and paw paw, scoop out seeds, then peel and dice flesh. Peel mango, pare flesh away from stone and cut into strips. Combine all fruits in bowl with grapefruit.

◆ Melt golden syrup, pour over fruits and mix gently. Spoon into grapefruit shells. Top each with a small knob of butter.

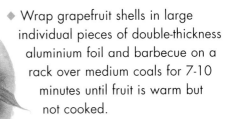

◆ Wrap grapefruit shells in large individual pieces of double-thickness aluminium foil and barbecue on a rack over medium coals for 7-10 minutes until fruit is warm but not cooked.

◆ Remove grapefruit from foil, place in individual dishes, top with toasted coconut and garnish with sprigs of mint.

Coconut Pineapple

SERVES 4

4 TABLESPOONS
DESICCATED COCONUT

1 PINEAPPLE

2 TABLESPOONS RUM

55G (2OZ) BROWN SUGAR

◆ Line a grill pan with aluminium foil and spread coconut over. Grill under a low heat, stirring frequently, until just toasted. Remove and set aside.

◆ Using a sharp knife, cut pineapple, lengthways, into 8 wedges, cutting through leaves and leaving them attached to the pineapple wedges. Cut away core. Sprinkle rum, then brown sugar, evenly over pineapple flesh.

◆ Place pineapple wedges on the barbecue over medium coals until sugar begins to caramelise and pineapple is hot and beginning to soften.

◆ Sprinkle over reserved toasted coconut to serve.

Bananas with Maple Syrup and Pecan Nuts

SERVES 4

*55G (2OZ) PECAN NUTS,
COARSELY CHOPPED*

6 TABLESPOONS MAPLE SYRUP

4 BANANAS

*VANILLA OR RUM AND RAISIN ICE CREAM,
TO SERVE (OPTIONAL)*

◆ Cook whole bananas in their skins on a prepared barbecue for 12-15 minutes, until skins are completely black and bananas are soft.

◆ Just before serving, gently warm pecan nuts and maple syrup in a saucepan over low heat.

◆ To serve, remove bananas from their skins and top with warm nutty syrup and scoops of ice cream, if desired.

Fruit Skewers with Chocolate Nut Sauce

SERVES 6

12 STRAWBERRIES

6 APRICOTS, HALVED

*3 PEARS, PEELED AND
CUT INTO QUARTERS*

2 TABLESPOONS CASTER SUGAR

CHOCOLATE NUT SAUCE

*115G (4OZ) MILK CHOCOLATE,
CHOPPED*

150ML (5FL OZ) SINGLE CREAM

*6 MARSHMALLOWS,
CHOPPED*

*25G (1OZ) SKINLESS HAZELNUTS,
TOASTED AND CHOPPED*

◆ To make sauce, melt chocolate, cream and marshmallows in a saucepan over low heat, stirring continually.

◆ Whisk to produce a smooth sauce and boil for 2 minutes to thicken. Stir in nuts and set sauce aside.

◆ Place strawberries, apricots and pears in a bowl, sprinkle over caster sugar and toss gently to coat. Divide fruit between skewers.

◆ Place fruit skewers on the barbecue and cook them for 5-6 minutes, turning frequently, until fruit is warmed through.

◆ Serve hot with chocolate nut sauce passed separately for dipping.

Walnut Apple Crescents

SERVES 4

4 TABLESPOONS APPLE JUICE

1 TEASPOON GRATED ORANGE PEEL

25G (1OZ) SHELLED WALNUTS, ROUGHLY CHOPPED

25G (1OZ) DATES, ROUGHLY CHOPPED

2 SMALL RED-SKINNED EATING APPLES

STRIPS ORANGE PEEL, TO GARNISH

◆ Place apple juice and grated orange peel in a small saucepan. Add walnuts and dates, bring to boil, then simmer for 2-3 minutes until liquid has been absorbed. Cool slightly.

◆ Rinse and dry apples and remove core, keeping apples whole. Cut each apple in half lengthways. (Each half will have a tubular-shaped hollow along its centre.)

◆ Fill apple hollows with fruit and nut mixture and wrap each apple half in double-thickness aluminium foil.

◆ Barbecue over hot coals for about 30 minutes, turning occasionally, until apples are tender. Garnish with strips of orange peel to serve.

Rum and Raisin Sharon Fruit

SERVES 6

6 FIRM SHARON FRUIT

25G (1OZ) MIXED DRIED FRUIT

1 GLACE CHERRY

3 UNSKINNED ALMONDS

2 TEASPOONS DARK SOFT BROWN SUGAR

1 TEASPOON DARK RUM

PINCH GROUND CINNAMON

½ TEASPOON LEMON JUICE

6 SMALL STRAWBERRIES, TO GARNISH

◆ Remove stalks from sharon fruit and, using a teaspoon, scoop out pulp, leaving fleshy wall intact. Place pulp in a bowl.

◆ Using a sharp, lightly floured knife, very finely chop dried fruit, glacé cherry and almonds. Mix into sharon fruit pulp, adding sugar, rum, cinnamon and lemon juice and stirring to combine.

◆ Carefully pack filling into sharon fruit shells and wrap each one separately in a piece of lightly oiled, double-thickness aluminium foil.

◆ Place foil parcels in medium coals and cook for 25-30 minutes until fruit is soft.

◆ To serve, unwrap parcels and top each one with a strawberry.

Praline Bananas

SERVES 6

6 UNDER-RIPE BANANAS

*WHIPPED CREAM,
TO SERVE*

PRALINE

1 TABLESPOON UNSKINNED ALMONDS

1 TABLESPOON UNSKINNED HAZELNUTS

55G (2OZ) GRANULATED SUGAR

◆ To make the praline, place almonds, hazelnuts and sugar in a small, heavy-based frying pan. Heat gently, stirring continually, until sugar dissolves. Raise heat and cook to a deep brown syrup.

◆ Immediately, pour this toffee-like mixture onto a sheet of non-stick baking parchment placed on a metal baking sheet on a wooden board. (It will be very hot.) Leave until cold and brittle, then crush finely.

◆ Lay unpeeled bananas flat and make a slit through the skin lengthways. Slightly open out the skin and fill each slit with about 3 teaspoons of praline.

◆ Re-shape bananas and wrap individually and tightly in double-thickness aluminium foil, sealing along the top.

◆ Barbecue banana parcels directly on medium coals for 8-10 minutes, turning them over halfway through cooking time.

◆ To serve, unfold foil wrapping and slightly open banana skins. Serve with whipped cream.

Exotic Fruit with Passion Fruit Dip

SERVES 4

1 SMALL RIPE PAW PAW

1 SMALL RIPE MANGO

2 BANANAS

2 THICK SLICES FRESH PINEAPPLE, HALVED

55G (2OZ) UNSALTED BUTTER, MELTED

2 TEASPOONS ICING SUGAR, SIFTED

PASSION FRUIT DIP

200ML (7FL OZ) CRÈME FRAÎCHE

1 TABLESPOON ICING SUGAR, SIFTED

PULP AND JUICE 3 PASSION FRUIT

MINT SPRIGS, TO DECORATE

◆ To make dip, mix together in a bowl crème fraîche, icing sugar and passion fruit pulp and juice. Cover and refrigerate until required.

◆ Cut the paw paw into 4 thick slices and seed. Cut the mango into quarters around the pit. Halve the bananas lengthways, but do not peel.

◆ Place paw paw and pineapple slices, mango quarters and banana halves on a large tray. Mix together melted butter and icing sugar, and brush mixture all over fruit.

◆ Cook all fruit on the barbecue, turning paw paw, mango and pineapple over occasionally until they begin to caramelise. The paw paw will take about 4 minutes to cook and the mango, pineapple and bananas about 6.

◆ Garnish with mint sprigs and serve fruit with dip.

Peach and Almond Dessert with Amaretto

SERVES 4

55G (2OZ) MADEIRA CAKE, CRUMBLED

6 AMARETTI BISCUITS, COARSELY CRUSHED

4 TABLESPOONS AMARETTO LIQUEUR

4 RIPE PEACHES, HALVED AND STONES REMOVED

25G (1OZ) FLAKED ALMONDS, TOASTED

8 TABLESPOONS FRESHLY SQUEEZED ORANGE JUICE

MASCARPONE CHEESE, TO SERVE

◆ Mix Madeira cake, amaretti biscuits and 2 tablespoons of Amaretto liqueur together in a bowl.

◆ Divide mixture between hollows of peaches. Sprinkle a few flaked almonds onto each peach half.

◆ Mix together remaining Amaretto liqueur and orange juice. Place 2 peach halves on a large piece of double-thickness aluminium foil. Spoon one quarter of the orange juice mixture over each peach and fold over foil to make a parcel. Repeat with remaining peaches.

◆ Cook peach parcels on the barbecue for about 10 minutes, until they are tender and warmed through. Serve with Mascarpone cheese.

Grand Marnier Kebabs

3 FIRM APRICOTS

3 FIRM FRESH FIGS

*2 PINEAPPLE SLICES,
EACH 2.5CM (1IN) THICK*

2 SATSUMAS

2 FIRM BANANAS

2 EATING APPLES

1 TABLESPOON LEMON JUICE

85G (3OZ) UNSALTED BUTTER

85G (3OZ) ICING SUGAR

1 TABLESPOON GRAND MARNIER

1 TABLESPOON FRESH ORANGE JUICE

*1 TABLESPOON FINELY GRATED
ORANGE ZEST*

◆ Halve apricots and remove stones. Remove stalks from figs and quarter lengthways. Remove and discard any woody core from pineapple slices, trim, and cut pineapple slices into chunks.

◆ Peel satsumas and quarter, but do not remove membranes. Peel bananas and cut into 2.5cm (1in) thick slices. Peel apples, cut into quarters, remove cores and halve each apple piece crossways. Sprinkle apples and bananas with lemon juice to prevent discoloration.

◆ Thread fruit onto 6-8 skewers, making sure that each has a mixture of fruit and starting and finishing with apple and pineapple.

◆ Melt butter, stir in icing sugar, then add Grand Marnier, orange juice and zest. Brush kebabs with sauce.

◆ Barbecue over medium coals for 5-6 minutes, frequently basting with sauce. Serve kebabs hot with any remaining sauce.

Peaches and Butterscotch

*6 PEACHES,
HALVED AND STONED*

55G (2OZ) GROUND ALMONDS

*3 TABLESPOONS FINELY CHOPPED
ANGELICA*

BUTTERSCOTCH SAUCE

*85G (3OZ) LIGHT SOFT
BROWN SUGAR*

150ML (5FL OZ) MAPLE SYRUP

45G (1½OZ) BUTTER

PINCH SALT

*150ML (5FL OZ) SINGLE
CREAM*

FEW DROPS VANILLA ESSENCE

◆ To make butterscotch sauce, combine sugar, maple syrup, butter and salt in a heavy-based saucepan. Bring to boil, stir once, then boil for 3 minutes to form a thick syrup.

◆ Stir in cream, bring back to boil and immediately remove from heat. Stir in vanilla essence to taste. Pour into a jug and keep warm.

◆ Place peach halves, cut sides down, on individual squares of double-thickness aluminium foil. Curl up sides of foil, but do not seal. Barbecue on rack over hot coals for 5 minutes.

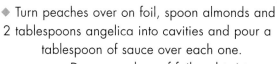

◆ Turn peaches over on foil, spoon almonds and 2 tablespoons angelica into cavities and pour a tablespoon of sauce over each one. Draw up edges of foil and twist above peaches to seal. Barbecue for 10 minutes until tender.

◆ Decorate with remaining angelica and serve hot with remaining sauce.

Vodka-soused Pineapple

*4 LARGE, FRESH PINEAPPLE SLICES,
EACH 2CM (1IN) THICK*

3 TABLESPOONS VODKA

85G (3OZ) UNSALTED BUTTER

55ML (2FL OZ) DOUBLE CREAM

1 TEASPOON GROUND CARDAMOM

2 TABLESPOONS ICING SUGAR

12 BOTTLED MORELLO CHERRIES

ICING SUGAR, FOR DUSTING

◆ Peel pineapple and remove central core. Pour vodka into a shallow dish, add pineapple slices, then turn slices over once. Cover dish and leave to marinate for 20 minutes.

◆ Melt butter in a small saucepan. Remove from heat and stir in cream, cardamom and icing sugar.

◆ Dip pineapple slices into melted butter mixture and barbecue on rack over hot coals for 5 minutes on each side until golden brown.

◆ Serve on warm plates, with pineapple centres filled with morello cherries. Dust lightly with icing sugar.

Tamarillos with Brown Sugar

SERVES 4

4 RIPE TAMARILLOS, HALVED

3 TABLESPOONS DEMERARA SUGAR

VANILLA ICE CREAM,
TO SERVE (OPTIONAL)

◆ Place 2 tamarillo halves on a piece of aluminium foil. Sprinkle with one quarter of the Demerara sugar and fold foil over to produce a parcel. Repeat with remaining tamarillos and sugar to produce 4 individual parcels.

◆ Cook tamarillo parcels on the barbecue for about 10 minutes, until they are warmed through and sugar has melted.

◆ Serve at once, with scoops of vanilla ice cream if desired.

Almond-stuffed Medjool Dates

SERVES 2-4

12 LARGE FRESH MEDJOOL DATES

85G (3OZ) BLANCHED ALMONDS,
TOASTED

2 TABLESPOONS MASCARPONE CHEESE
OR CREAM CHEESE

4 TABLESPOONS BRANDY

1 CINNAMON STICK,
BROKEN IN HALF

2 TABLESPOONS SOFT BROWN SUGAR

4 TABLESPOONS FRESHLY SQUEEZED
ORANGE JUICE

GREEK YOGHURT,
TO SERVE

◆ Make a slit in the side of each date and remove and discard stones. Reserve 12 whole blanched almonds and finely chop the remainder.

◆ Place chopped almonds in a bowl and add mascarpone cheese and 2 tablespoons brandy. Mix well to combine. Fill dates with mixture and add a whole almond to each cavity.

◆ Place 6 dates and half a cinnamon stick on a large piece of double-thickness aluminium foil.

◆ Mix remaining brandy, brown sugar and orange juice together. Spoon half of the mixture over the dates.

◆ Wrap up foil to produce a parcel. Repeat with remaining dates, cinnamon and orange juice mixture.

◆ Cook foil parcels on the barbecue for about 10 minutes, until dates are tender and warmed through. Serve with yoghurt.

Pear with Chocolate Sauce

SERVES 4

115G (4OZ) RICOTTA CHEESE

55G (2OZ) GROUND HAZELNUTS

2 TABLESPOONS CLEAR HONEY

2 SMALL EGG YOLKS

SEEDS FROM 1 CARDAMOM POD, CRUSHED

4 LARGE PEARS

CHOCOLATE SAUCE

115G (4OZ) PLAIN CHOCOLATE

45G (1½OZ) UNSALTED BUTTER

2 TABLESPOONS BRANDY

2 TABLESPOONS THICK SOUR CREAM

◆ Cream together ricotta cheese, ground hazelnuts, honey, egg yolks and crushed cardamom seeds.

◆ Peel pears. Cut a thin slice from base of each pear and, using a corer or small spoon, carefully scoop out core as far up inside the pear as possible, without damaging the flesh.

◆ Fill cavities with ricotta mixture, pressing in well. Smooth bases flat. Place pears on individual pieces of double-thickness aluminium foil and twist at the tops to secure fillings.

◆ Place on the barbecue rack over medium coals for 20-30 minutes until pears are cooked.

◆ Just before pears are ready, make sauce. Place chocolate, butter, brandy and thick sour cream in a small pan and heat gently until melted. Stir well and keep warm.

◆ Transfer pears to serving plates, slice in half to reveal filling and pour over sauce. Serve immediately.

Dips and Sauces

Avocado and Chilli Dip

SERVES 4

1 FAT GREEN FRESH CHILLI

2 MEDIUM-SIZED RIPE AVOCADOS

GRATED ZEST 1 LIME

1 TABLESPOON LIME JUICE

3 TABLESPOONS FINELY CHOPPED MIXED FRESH HERBS (E.G. LOVAGE, ROCKET, SORREL, SAVORY, THYME, PARSLEY, BASIL, CHIVES, TARRAGON)

85G (3OZ) RICOTTA CHEESE

1 GARLIC CLOVE, CRUSHED

2 TEASPOONS GREEN PEPPERCORNS, CRUSHED

¼ TEASPOON COARSE SEA SALT

HERB SPRIGS, TO GARNISH

◆ Place chilli on the barbecue rack over hot coals for 5-8 minutes, turning frequently, until skin blisters and blackens. Remove skin and seeds and chop flesh roughly.

◆ Peel avocados and chop flesh roughly. Mix with lime juice to prevent discoloration.

◆ Place avocado in a blender or food processor with chilli, lime zest, fresh herbs, ricotta cheese, garlic, green peppercorns and sea salt and blend until smooth. Season to taste, adding more lime juice if necessary.

◆ Pour or spoon dip into a serving bowl and garnish with sprigs of herbs. If not serving immediately, sprinkle with lime juice, cover tightly with plastic wrap and chill in the refrigerator.

Chargrilled Tomato and Chilli Sauce

SERVES 4

900G (2LB) PLUM TOMATOES

*4 LARGE GARLIC CLOVES,
UNPEELED*

2 FRESH GREEN CHILLIES

2 TEASPOONS DRIED OREGANO OR THYME

2 TABLESPOONS OLIVE OIL

½ ONION, FINELY CHOPPED

½ TEASPOON SUGAR

½ TEASPOON SALT

FRESHLY GROUND BLACK PEPPER

15G (½ OZ) BUTTER

◆ Place tomatoes, garlic and chillies on the barbecue over hot coals. Turn frequently, until skins blister and blacken. (Chillies will need about 5 minutes, garlic 10 minutes and tomatoes 15 minutes.)

◆ Peel garlic, remove skin and seeds from chilli, but do not peel tomatoes.

◆ Dry-fry oregano in a small heavy-based pan for a few minutes until you can smell the aroma.

◆ Heat oil in another small pan. Gently fry onion for about 5 minutes until translucent. Add oregano and fry for another minute.

◆ Purée tomatoes, including any blackened bits of skin (they add to the flavour), with garlic, chilli and onion mixture until smooth.

◆ Pour into a large frying pan and season with sugar, salt and freshly ground black pepper. Simmer for 5-10 minutes, stirring occasionally, until some of the liquid has evaporated. Stir in butter.

Skordalia

**MAKES ABOUT
225ml (8fl oz)**

*2 SLICES DAY-OLD WHITE BREAD,
CUBED*

55ML (2FL OZ) MILK

2 GARLIC CLOVES, CRUSHED

2 TEASPOONS SEA SALT

PINCH CAYENNE PEPPER

85ML (3FL OZ) EXTRA VIRGIN OLIVE OIL

1 TABLESPOON LEMON JUICE

◆ Soak bread in milk for 5 minutes. Squeeze out milk and place bread in a blender or food processor. Add garlic, sea salt and cayenne pepper and blend until smooth.

◆ Gradually blend in oil and 1 tablespoon boiling water to form a thick sauce. Stir in lemon juice and season to taste.

◆ Refrigerate and use within two days.

Olive and Coriander Relish

SERVES 4

2 RED PEPPERS

*175G (6OZ) BLACK OLIVES IN OIL,
STONED AND SLICED FINELY*

*½ FRESH GREEN CHILLI,
SEEDED AND VERY FINELY CHOPPED*

*6 TABLESPOONS FINELY CHOPPED
CORIANDER LEAVES*

1 TABLESPOON LEMON JUICE

FRESHLY GROUND BLACK PEPPER

5 TABLESPOONS OLIVE OIL

LETTUCE LEAVES, TO SERVE

*1 HARD-BOILED EGG,
QUARTERED, TO SERVE*

◆ Place peppers on the barbecue over hot coals for 10 minutes, turning occasionally, until skins begin to blacken. Cover or place in a sealed plastic bag for 5 minutes.

◆ Remove skin and seeds and cut flesh into small dice. Mix with olives, chilli and coriander in a bowl.

◆ Whisk together lemon juice, freshly ground black pepper and olive oil and pour over olive mixture. Allow to stand at room temperature for 1 hour.

◆ Pile mixture on a bed of lettuce leaves and top with hard-boiled egg quarters to serve.

Chickpea and Aubergine Dip

SERVES 4

2 SMALL AUBERGINES

85G (3OZ) CHICKPEAS,
SOAKED OVERNIGHT

¼ TEASPOON SALT

6 TABLESPOONS GREEK YOGHURT

GRATED ZEST ½ LIME

2 TABLESPOONS LIME JUICE

1 GARLIC CLOVE, CRUSHED

2 TABLESPOONS OLIVE OIL

PINCH CAYENNE PEPPER

BLACK OLIVES, TO GARNISH

PINCH CAYENNE PEPPER,
TO GARNISH

◆ Cook aubergines on barbecue over hot coals for 15-20 minutes, turning occasionally until charred. Allow to cool slightly, then remove skin. Squeeze out bitter juices then leave to drain.

◆ Place chickpeas in large saucepan of water. Bring to boil and simmer for about 20 minutes until soft. Add salt halfway through cooking time.

◆ Drain and purée chickpeas in a blender or food processor with aubergines, yoghurt, lime zest and juice, garlic, olive oil, and cayenne pepper until smooth.

◆ Transfer to a bowl and garnish with olives and cayenne pepper.

Roasted Red Pepper Sauce

MAKES ABOUT
700ml (1½ PINTS)

3 RED PEPPERS

3 ORANGE PEPPERS

3 TABLESPOONS OLIVE OIL

4 SHALLOTS, CHOPPED

2 GARLIC CLOVES, CRUSHED

300ML (½ PINT) VEGETABLE STOCK

1 TABLESPOON RED WINE VINEGAR

1 TEASPOON CASTER SUGAR

SALT AND FRESHLY GROUND BLACK PEPPER

◆ Cook peppers over hot coals for 10 minutes, turning occasionally, until skins begin to blacken.

◆ Cover or place in a sealed plastic bag for 5 minutes. Peel away skin, remove seeds and chop flesh coarsely.

◆ Heat oil in a pan and sauté shallots and garlic for 4-5 minutes until softened.

◆ Add peppers, stock, vinegar, sugar and seasoning, and cook mixture, uncovered, for 10-15 minutes until liquid has reduced slightly.

◆ Allow mixture to cool and then purée in a blender or food processor to produce a smooth, thick sauce. Taste and adjust seasoning if necessary.

◆ The sauce will keep fresh for 4-5 days stored in the refrigerator.

Spicy Tomato Sauce

MAKES ABOUT
850ml (1½ PINTS)

900G (2LB) RIPE TOMATOES

3 GARLIC CLOVES, UNPEELED

3 TABLESPOONS OLIVE OIL

3-4 FRESH RED CHILLIES,
SEEDED AND FINELY CHOPPED

2 SHALLOTS, FINELY CHOPPED

1 TEASPOON CASTER SUGAR

SALT AND FRESHLY GROUND BLACK PEPPER

◆ Cook tomatoes and garlic cloves on the rack over medium coals, turning occasionally, for about 10 minutes. The tomatoes are ready when they have softened and their skins begin to char. The garlic should be browned and soft.

◆ Remove tomatoes and garlic cloves from the grill and allow to cool. Peel garlic and mash flesh. Do not peel tomatoes, but chop roughly.

◆ Heat oil in a saucepan and add chillies and shallots. Cook for 5 minutes. Add tomatoes, garlic, sugar and salt and pepper to the pan and stir, uncovered, for 15 minutes, until the sauce is thick.

◆ Allow the sauce to cool, then purée it in a blender or food processor until smooth. Taste and adjust seasoning as necessary.

◆ The sauce will keep fresh for 4-5 days stored in the refrigerator. It makes the perfect pizza topping or a sauce for calzone.

Grilled Corn Salsa

2 LARGE SWEETCORN

*1 RED OR LARGE SWEET ONION,
FINELY CHOPPED*

*4 RIPE PLUM TOMATOES,
SEEDED AND COARSELY CHOPPED*

1 GARLIC CLOVE, FINELY CHOPPED

*2 JALAPINO CHILLIES,
SEEDED AND FINELY CHOPPED*

*1 BUNCH CORIANDER,
TRIMMED AND FINELY CHOPPED*

SALT AND FRESHLY GROUND BLACK PEPPER

◆ Cook sweetcorn in plenty of boiling water for about 15 minutes, until tender. Drain.

◆ Place sweetcorn on rack of barbecue over hot coals and cook, turning occasionally, for about 10 minutes. Leave to cool.

◆ Hold sweetcorn vertically at a slight angle to the chopping board, stem end down. Using a sharp knife, cut down along cob to remove kernels. Place kernels in a large bowl and repeat with remaining sweetcorn.

◆ Using a sharp knife, scrape along each cob, removing remaining 'milk' and add this to the bowl. Stir in onion.

◆ Add tomatoes, garlic, chillies, coriander, salt and black pepper. Toss together and spoon into a serving bowl.

◆ Leave to stand for about 30 minutes before serving.

Baba Ganoush

SERVES 6

2 SMALL AUBERGINES

1 GARLIC CLOVE, CRUSHED

4 TABLESPOONS TAHINI

25G (1OZ) GROUND ALMONDS

JUICE ½ LEMON

½ TEASPOON GROUND CUMIN

SALT AND FRESHLY GROUND BLACK PEPPER

1 TABLESPOON CHOPPED FRESH MINT

2 TABLESPOONS OLIVE OIL

FRESH MINT LEAVES, TO GARNISH

SELECTION OF VEGETABLES, SUCH AS BABY ARTICHOKES, RADISHES, SLICED PEPPERS, TO SERVE

◆ Cook aubergines on a rack over hot coals, turning often, until black and blistered.

◆ Remove skins, chop flesh roughly and leave to drain in a colander for 10 minutes.

◆ Squeeze out as much liquid from aubergines as possible and place flesh in a food processor or blender.

◆ Add garlic, tahini, ground almonds, lemon juice, cumin, salt and freshly ground black pepper and process to a smooth paste. Stir chopped mint leaves into dip.

◆ Spoon into a bowl and drizzle with olive oil. Scatter mint leaves on top. Place bowl on a serving platter and serve with a selection of vegetables.

Index